COPYCAT RECIPES

An Easy Step-by-Step Guide to Make Your Cracker Barrel's Most Favorite Recipes at Home on a Budget. Includes Delicious Keto Recipes to Enjoy with your Family and Friends

LISA JOHNSON

LISA JOHNSON

TABLE OF CONTENTS

INTRODUCTION

Copycat recipes are very popular these days, and for good reason. They're quick, easy, and provide a great meal for the family or a quick appetizer for friends. Copycat recipes are a prodigious method to get a sense of how something tastes like deprived of having to fill a lot of money on ingredients. When you're looking for a new recipe, try out a copycat recipe version from one of your favorite chefs that you can substitute for the traditional recipe. You can also taste these recipes at home and then decide if they are something you want to make at home. You don't have to buy the expensive ingredients unless you are certain that you really love it, but there are periods when it is best to save money by using cheaper substitutes for things that you need to do.

You don't need special ingredients for some copycat recipes because you can buy a lot of the similar effects at the grocery store and use them for many different meals. If you compare two similar recipes, buy the recipe and try it out before you decide if it is something that is worth making at home. You might even discover that you like it even better than the original recipe.

To ensure you're making the same restaurant dishes, copycat recipes are continuously checked. Chefs with a lot of experience spend hours tweaking these recipes to get the perfect taste. Such recipes are as authentic as those found in your favorite restaurant's kitchen. What's the perfect way to save money on these bogus recipes?

The amount of money you save with these recipes would be astounding. Imagine enjoying an evening with your partner at your favorite restaurant. You'll get an appetizer, two appetizers, and a cake to share. You easily spent between $ 55 and $ 70 on drinks, snacks, and tips. You can possibly make these recipes at home for about a third of the price without sacrificing flavor. As a result, you can use copycat recipes to make three separate meals at home, making it impossible to eat only one meal. So, where do you think you'll find these recipes?

The greatest of the counterfeit recipes is this one. You won't need any unusual ingredients or kitchen utensils. You perhaps already have the whole thing you need in your pantry if you're cooking. What you don't have should be available at your local store right away. It isn't exotic in the least.

Recall the last period you dined at your favorite eatery. Is there a dividing line? How eagerly did you expect your favorite meal to come when you sat down? When the server sited it on the table, I got that feeling. Was it, in the end, perfect? Or not; as though it wasn't fully cooked. Or did they leave a cover because it wasn't hot enough? When you first got this account, how did you feel? Is "Aahhh" now "woooah?" I'll show you how to avoid these food-related issues. It's all about using tried-and-true imitation recipes. Do you want to know the top five reasons why you should make your favorite home-cooked meal?

How much money will you save if you use fake recipes? Let's say you and your girlfriend go out to dinner. Let's finish with some drinks and a suggestion. You've easily spent between $ 60 and $ 80 anywhere in the neighborhood. You will receive an appetizer, two outings, and probably a dessert split. You could have had the same meal for $25-$30 at home, which is less than half the price! Meanwhile, you won't be missing out on any taste. In these difficult economic times, this is a big savings.

Making imitated home recipes is good for your health. It will either give your food a new taste or it will add your vegetables.

These recipes were developed by a group of experienced chefs. We've double-checked that you have all of the required ingredients and directions to prepare your favorite meal.

Eleftheria: Do you understand how much food you waste in your spare time? Is it possible to get the lunch you want? Will you eat your favorite food while watching your favorite show? Driving to a restaurant, waiting to be seated, waiting for your appetizer, waiting for your dinner, waiting for your dessert, and, of course, waiting to pay your bill. So, how long have you been anticipating this moment? Two or three hours more? Reclaim your time and independence by preparing your favorite meals at home. When you want to cook your favorite food the way you want, use these imitation recipes.

MAKING CRACKER BARREL'S MOST POPULAR RECIPES

Cracker Barrel is America's most famous home of "good ol' southern cooking". This restaurant chain has been in the business for over 50 years and satisfies all your Southern cravings with their classic recipes.

Cracker Barrel has been around for over 40 years, and in that time they have served some of the best fried chicken, biscuits, and pecan pie you will ever find. Across the country, there are over 500 locations — but if you don't live near one, you may be wondering how to enjoy these dishes in your own kitchen. It's not always easy to recreate the flavors of Cracker Barrel at home , since many of their recipes and ingredients are proprietary to the restaurant chain. But that doesn't mean it's impossible — you can make some of your favorite Cracker Barrel recipes at home.

THE KETO VERSION OF CRACKER BARREL'S

The Keto Crack Barrel is a high-protein, low-carb breakfast option enjoyed by millions of people with all sorts of lifestyles. It's perfect for those on a ketogenic diet to enjoy before dinner, or even as a quick meal while at work.

The Keto Crack Barrel includes a medium or large breakfast with egg, sausage, cheese, and a slice of ham or bacon—and of course a side of grits. While the typical meal contains between 1,400-1,800 calories, you can stay within the limits of your ketogenic diet by omitting the grits and limiting yourself to just one slice of bread.

The first time you try one of these things, it will immediately become your favorite food in the world. Cracker Barrel is popular for their delicious, homemade meals and scrumptious desserts you'll want to try. Most of the food items there are cooked with fresh ingredients.

For breakfast, they offer french toast, cornbread, and pancakes. For lunch, there are a variety of soups and sandwich options along with their famous meatloaf.

Their dinner menu includes seafood dishes as well as many meat dishes. Their popular desserts are their sweet-potato casserole, coconut pie, and bread pudding. Cracker Barrel is a community favorite as they participate in local events and offer local products that are sold within their store.

Examples includes : Blueberry pancakes from ihop, Blueberry muffins from starbucks, Glazed donuts from krispy kreme, Biscuits and sausage gravy from bob evans, Sweet potato pancakes from cracker barrel When it comes to eating the keto diet way, Cracker Barrel should not be your first preference, but it has come a long way since it first became famous years ago.

There wasn't anything on the menu back then that wasn't deep fried or smothered in gravy. Low-carb dieters now have a variety of meal choices.

Keep in mind that while Cracker Barrel or some other restaurant may have something low carb, it won't meet your strict keto requirements.

It is still preferable to do your own grocery shopping and meal preparation at home. This gives you full control over the ingredients you're using in your cooking. Try to reduce your eating out to once or twice a month.

If you find yourself in a position where you have no choice but to eat at Cracker Barrel, use these tips to help you make a wise food choice.

Cracker Barrel Dining Recommendations

Since Cracker Barrel is based in Tennessee, most of their dishes have a southern flair.

Expect a lot of strong side dishes like macaroni and cheese, mashed potatoes and gravy, and dumplings if you've never been to the south before. Sure, they're delicious, but they don't quite fulfill the low-carb criteria.

You may be able to satisfy your hunger with a bunless bacon cheeseburger from Cracker Barrel, but your meats and cheeses are likely to have been raised in a traditional setting and pumped full of hormones, antibiotics, added sugars, and nitrates/nitrites.

Furthermore, fast food would most likely be cooked with low-cost vegetable oils rather than high-quality avocado, coconut, or olive oil.

The good news is that the menu includes some nutritious options, such as steamed broccoli and boiled cabbage. The trick is to avoid buying the wrong thing and ruining your meal.

If you take the steps below, you'll be able to eat low-carb at Cracker Barrel.

Before you go, take a peek at their menu.

Cracker Barrel can require you to approach it as though you were studying for an exam. Eating out on a ketogenic diet is a challenge in several respects.

You can either pass or fail the exam. If you don't succeed, you can be kicked out of ketosis. However, if you do it well, you will be able to enjoy a meal out now and then without jeopardizing all of your hard work.

We recommend going at the Cracker Barrel menu ahead of time so you know what to order when you arrive. You can consume all of your meals or snacks here and most locations are open from 6 a.m. to 10 p.m.

They have a lighter twist menu of calorie-counted meals, but you'll always need to tweak them to make them low-carb.

Make a breakfast order

Cracker Barrel serves breakfast all day. This is fantastic news because it's one of the simplest low-carb diets to follow.

Simply order eggs, bacon, and cheese, and you're ready to go. Request a side of sausage or ham instead of the bread, fruit juice, and hash browns that come with your meal.

An omelet or over-easy eggs are your best choice. This is due because many restaurants use milk to make their scrambled eggs light and fluffy. Remember when next you go to a breakfast buffet. Some restaurants add milk to omelets as well, so make sure to specify that you don't want it.

For added fiber and antioxidants, top your omelet with low-carb veggies like spinach, onions, and mushrooms.

Don't eat the occasional specials.

Your server will most likely hand you a separate menu with the regular specials when you visit a Cracker Barrel restaurant. Don't get too worked up about them. Specials are tempting, but they are for food that you don't need or can't consume on a low-carb diet.

On Monday through Friday, for example, you can get a pick two combo at Cracker Barrel for just $5.99, but your choices include a grilled cheese sandwich, a baked potato, and a cup of soup.

Meatloaf with mashed potatoes, chicken pot pie, and fish fry are among the other regular specials. Since none of these are low-carb, stick to the standard menu.

Furthermore, specials are often prepared ahead of time. They become inaccessible when the restaurant runs out of them. This means they'll be less likely to make changes to your order. As a result, you won't be able to request no gravy or a different side dish that isn't deep fried.

CHAPTER 1

BREAKFAST

CRACKER BARREL APPLE STREUSEL FRENCH TOAST

Preparation Time 5 minutes **Cooking time** 30 minutes **Servings** 4
Ingredients
2½ cups Bisquick baking mix
2 teaspoons apple pie spice
½ cup flour
4 beaten eggs
1 cup apple sauce
1 (21ounce) can apple pie filling
¾ cup brown sugar
2 eggs
2/3 cup cooking oil
Directions
1. Preheat oven to 350 degrees. Grease and flour 2 small loaf pans.
2. Combine baking mixture, flour, and apple pie spice into a large bowl.
3. Combine apple sauce, 4 eggs, apple pie filling, 1/2 cup brown sugar, and oil into another large bowl. Attach this mixture to flour and whisk until moistened.
4. Equally divide batter between prepared pans. Top each loaf with remaining brown sugar.
5. Bake for about 55–60 minutes, or up until a toothpick inserted in the middle comes out clean.
6. Cool down for 10 minutes in pans on wire rack. Remove from the pans and fully cool on the wire rack. Wrap and store for easier slicing, overnight Beat the 2 eggs, in a small bowl. Break the bread into thick slices. Dip each bread slice into the egg. Fry to each side on a griddle until golden brown.
Nutrition: Calories 189, Fat 11.6, Fiber 3.4,Carbs 7.9 Protein 17.2

CRACKER BARREL PANCAKES

Preparation time: 10 minutes **Cooking time**: 15 minutes
Serving: 2
Ingredients
1 cup allpurpose flour
1/2 teaspoon baking soda
3/4 teaspoon baking powder
1/2 teaspoon salt
1 cup buttermilk
Two tablespoons butter, melted
One egg
Extra butter, for the griddle
Pure maple syrup
Directions:
In a big bowl, add the flour, baking powder, baking soda, and salt. I suggest using an electric mixer in a smaller bowl whisk the egg. Add buttermilk and the butter melted.
Blend in buttermilk egg mixture with dry ingredients until the batter gets smooth. Run a stick of butter over a warmed grid (or a big, flat frying pan). That is going to scorch the pancakes and your face.
For larger pancakes close to Cracker Barrel's, pour each pancake on a 1/2 cup batter (makes about 5). If you want smaller pancakes, pour on a 1/4 cup batter for each pancake (it will make about 10). Serve with Crack Barrel maple syrup and butter.
Nutrition: calories 170, fat 8, fiber 2, carbs 8, protein 4

BUTTERMILK PANCAKES

Preparation Time: 10 minutes
Cooking time: 15 minutes
Servings: 4
Ingredients:

- 2 cups un-sifted flour
- 2 teaspoons baking soda
- 1 teaspoon salt
- 3 tablespoons sugar
- 2 eggs
- 2⅓ cups low-fat buttermilk
- Butter for cooking

Directions:

1. Preheat a griddle or large skillet to 350°F.
2. Place a stick of butter close to the skillet; you will butter it before preparing each pancake.
3. In a medium bowl, whisk together the eggs and buttermilk until they are well combined. Whisk in the flour, baking soda, sugar, and salt. Whisk thoroughly until well combined.
4. Prepare the skillet by rubbing the butter in a circle in the center, then add about ½ cup of batter. Spread the batter until it forms an even circle.
5. When the pancake surface turns bubbly, flip and cook on the other side until you can't see wet spots on the sides.
6. Repeat with the remaining batter, making sure to butter the skillet before you start each pancake.
7. Serve with your favorite syrup or fruit.

Nutrition:
Calories 212
Protein 25
Carbs 16
Fat 5

Ham and Swiss Omelet

Preparation Time: 20 minutes
Cooking Time: 10 minutes
Serving: 1

Ingredients

- 1 tablespoon butter
- 3 eggs
- 3 tbsps. water
- 1/8 teaspoon sodium
- 1/8 teaspoon pepper
- 1/2 cup cubed fully cooked ham
- 1/4 cup cut Swiss cheese

Directions

1. In a little nonstick skillet, liquefy butter over medium-high warm. Blend the eggs, pepper, water and sodium. Add egg mixture to skillet (mixture must set quickly at edges).
2. As eggs prepared, press cooked sides toward the midpoint, allowing raw section circulation below.
3. When the eggs are established, place ham on one edge and sprinkle with cheese; fold opposite over filling. Slide omelet onto a layer.

Nutrition
530 calories
726mg cholesterol
4g carbohydrate

CRACKER BARREL FRENCH TOAST

Preparation Time: 1 minutes
Cooking Time: 5 minutes
Servings: 1
Ingredients:

- 8 slices Texas Toast (or Sourdough bread)
- 4 eggs
- 1 cup Milk
- 2 Tablespoons Sugar
- 4 teaspoons Vanilla extract
- 2 pinches of salt

Directions:

1. Incorporate eggs, milk, sugar, vanilla, and salt together in a large bowl.
2. Preheat griddle to 350F. Brush with butter/margarine.
3. Submerge the slice of bread in egg mixture for 30 seconds on each side.
4. Situate slices on griddle and cook for 4-5 minutes, or until golden brown.
5. Side with a pat of butter and your favorite syrup!

Nutrition:
1312 Calories
30.5g Total fat
191g Carbohydrates
54.1g Protein

EGG MCMUFFINS

Preparation Time: 5 minutes
Cooking Time: 10 minutes
Servings: 2
Ingredients:

- 1 tablespoon unsalted butter
- 1 English muffin
- 1 slice high-quality Canadian bacon
- 1 large egg
- 1 slice Swiss, or Jack cheese

Direction:

1. Spread 1 tsp. butter on each halves of English muffin and situate halves in a 10-inch nonstick at medium heat. Cook, then pressing gently to get good contact with pan for 4 minutes. Situate to a sheet of aluminum foil, split side up.
2. Cook remaining 1 teaspoon butter in the now-empty skillet and increase heat to medium-high. Fry bacon for 1 1/2 minutes. Situate bacon to lower muffin half.
3. Situate lid of a quart-sized, wide-mouthed Mason jar upside down in the now-empty skillet. Brush the inside with nonstick cooking spray and break egg into it. Prick the egg yolk with a fork to break it and season with salt and pepper. Stir in 3/4 cup (180ml) water into the skillet, cover, and cook until egg is set, about 2 minutes.
4. Using a thin spatula, situate Mason jar lid to a paper towel–lined plate. Take excess water out of the skillet and put it back to the stovetop with the heat off. Turn Mason jar lid over then gently remove it to release egg. Situate egg on top of bacon and garnish with cheese slice. Wrap with aluminum foil, and place it back to the now-empty skillet. Heat up in the skillet for 2 minutes with the heat off. Unwrap and serve immediately.

Nutrition:
96 Calories
12.8g Carbohydrates
5.3g Protein

PUMPKIN PANCAKES

Preparation Time: 10 minutes
Cooking Time: 10 minutes
Servings: 9
Ingredients:

- 1 ½ cups milk
- 1 cup pumpkin puree
- 1 egg
- 2 tablespoons vegetable oil
- 2 tablespoons vinegar
- 2 cups all-purpose flour
- 3 tablespoons brown sugar
- 2 teaspoons baking powder
- 1 teaspoon baking soda
- 1 teaspoon ground allspice
- 1 teaspoon ground cinnamon
- ½ teaspoon ground ginger
- ½ teaspoon salt

Directions:

1. Scourge milk, pumpkin, egg, oil and vinegar. Incorporate flour, brown sugar, baking powder, baking soda, allspice, cinnamon, ginger and salt in a separate bowl. Mix into the pumpkin mixture just enough to combine.
2. Preheat lightly oiled griddle or frying pan over medium high heat. Spoon batter onto the griddle, using approximately 1/4 cup for each pancake.

Nutrition:
134 Calories
5g Total fat
18g Carbohydrates

CRACKER BARREL'S BISCUITS

Preparation Time: 15 minutes
Cooking Time: 8 minutes
Servings: 8
Ingredients:
2 cups selfrising flour
⅓ cup shortening
⅔ cup buttermilk
Melted butter, to brush
Directions:
Preheat oven to 450 °F.
In a bowl, mix flour and shortening until mixture is loose and crumbly.
Pour in buttermilk. Mix well.
Sprinkle flour onto a smooth surface and flatten dough on top. Cut dough into desired shapes using biscuit cutters.
Arrange onto a baking sheet. Place in oven and cook for 8 minutes. Apply melted butter on top using a brush.
Serve.
Nutrition: Calories: 194 Fat: 9 g Carbs: 24 g Protein: 4 g Sodium: 418 mg

CRACKER BARREL™ COPYCAT EGG IN A BASKET

Preparation time: 10 minutes
Cooking time: 35 minutes
Serving: 2
Ingredients:
Margarine/butter (1 tbsp.)
Egg (1)
Sourdough bread (1 slic e)
Black pepper and salt (to your liking)
Directions:
Warm a skillet over medium heat. Use a small biscuit cutter to prepare the bread.
Spread butter on both sides of the bread and arrange in the pan.
To prepare an overeasy egg, toast the bread and drop the cracked egg into the ring as soon as you put the bread into the pan.
Otherwise, cook for about a minute before flipping the bread over onto the other side. Cook until the egg is the way you like it.
Nutrition: Calories: 441 fat: 20g Carbs: 63g Fiber: 13g Protein: 10g

SWEET POTATO PANCAKES FROM CRACKER BARREL
Preparation Time: 10 minutes
Cooking Time: 30 minutes
Servings: 8
Ingredients:

-
- One cubed sweet potato
- Half cup of milk
- Three eggs
- A quarter cup of flax seeds
- Half cup of oats (grind to flour)
- Half tsp. of baking powder
- Two scoops of protein powder (vanilla)
- A large-sized banana (sliced)
- Two tsps. of pumpkin pie spice
- Two tbsps. of coconut oil (use as required)
- Two and a half tbsps. each of

Walnuts
Pecans
Almonds
Directions:
1. Take a clean pot and fill it up with fresh water. Let the water boil and then stir in the cubed sweet potatoes. Cook for a minimum time of seven-ten minutes so that the sweet potatoes become tender enough. Drain the water.
2. Next, you need a fork and a small bowl for mashing the potatoes.
3. Once your mashing is done, mix eggs, a cup of mashed sweet potatoes, oat flour, milk, flax seeds, protein powder, baking powder, pumpkin pie spice in a medium-sized bowl. After mixing evenly, stir in almonds, walnuts, pecans and banana slices until the batter is well combined.
4. Now it is time to melt the coconut oil using a skillet on medium heat. For making a four-six-inch-thick pancake, pour the required amount of batter into the skillet. Flip the pancake once. Cook each side for three-five minutes until it is golden brown.

Nutrition:
Calories: | Carbs: | Fat: | Protein: | Fiber:
Total Prep & Cooking Time: 33 minutes
Yields: 8 servings
Nutrition Facts: Calories: 240.5 | Protein: 15.5g | Carbs: 19g | Fat: 12.4g | Fiber: 4g

CHAPTER 2

SIDES AND SALADS

CRACKER BARREL'S BREADED FRIED OKRA
Preparation Time: 10 Minutes
Cooking time: 30 Minutes
Servings: 2
Ingredients:

- 1 Pound fresh okra, rinsed and dried
- 1 Cup self-rising cornmeal
- ½ Cup self-rising flour
- 1 Teaspoon salt
- 1 Cup vegetable oil (for frying)
- Salt and pepper to taste

Directions:

1. In a big skillet or deep fryer, heat the oil.
2. Cut the okra into 12-inch bits with a sharp knife.
3. In a big mixing bowl, combine the cornmeal, flour, and salt.
4. Throw the okra pieces in the bowl to cover them. Allow for a few minutes of resting while the oil heats up.
5. 5. Move the okra from the bowl to the hot oil with a slotted spoon.
6. Cook for around 10 minutes, or until the okra is golden in color.Remove from oil and place on a plate lined with paper towels to drain. Season to taste with salt and pepper.

Nutrition:

- Calories: 318
- Total Fat: 90g
- Carbs 6g
- Protein: 39g

CHICKEN POT STICKERS

Preparation Time: 40 Minutes
Cooking Time: 30 Minutes
Servings: 50
Ingredients:

- ½ Cup + 2 Tablespoons soy sauce, divided
- 1 tablespoon rice vinegar
- 3 tablespoons chives, divided
- 1 tablespoon sesame seeds
- 1 Teaspoon sriracha hot sauce
- 1-pound ground pork
- 3 cloves garlic, minced
- 1 egg, beaten
- 11/2tablespoons sesame oil
- 1 tablespoon fresh ginger, minced
- 50 dumpling wrappers
- 1 cup vegetable oil, for frying
- 1-quart water

Directions:

1. In a mixing bowl, whisk together the 1/2cup of soy sauce, vinegar, and 1 tablespoon of the chives, sesame seeds and sriracha to make the dipping sauce.
2. In a separate bowl, mix together the pork, garlic, egg, the rest of the chives, the 2 Tablespoons of soy sauce, sesame oil and the ginger.
3. Add about 1 tablespoon of the filling to each dumpling wrapper. Pinch the sides of the wrappers together to seal. You may need to wet the edges a bit so that they will stick.
4. Heat the cup of oil in a large skillet. When hot, working in batches, add the dumplings and cook until golden brown on all sides. Take care of not overloading your pan.
5. Add the water and cook until tender, then serve with the dipping sauce.

Nutrition:
Calories: : 140
Total Fat: 5 g
Cholesterol: 15 mg
Sodium: : 470mg
Total Carbohydrate: 9 g
Dietary Fiber: 1 g
Sugar: : 2 g
Protein: 6 g

CRACKER BARREL'S LETTUCE WRAPS

Preparation Time: 10 Minutes
Cooking Time: 10 Minutes
Servings: 4
Ingredients:

- 1 tablespoon olive oil
- 2 green onions, thinly sliced
- 1-pound ground chicken
- Kosher salt and ground black pepper to taste
- 2 cloves garlic, minced
- 1 onion, diced ¼ Cup hoisin sauce
- 1 tablespoon Sriracha (optional)
- 2 Tablespoons soy sauce
- 1 tablespoon rice wine vinegar
- 1 tablespoon ginger, freshly grated
- 1 (8-ounce) can whole water chestnuts, diced and drained
- 1 head iceberg lettuce

Directions:

1. Add the oil to a deep skillet or saucepan and heat over medium-high heat.
2. When hot, add the chicken and cook until it is completely cooked through.
3. Stir while cooking to make sure it is properly crumbled.
4. Drain any excess fat from the skillet, then add the garlic, onion, hoisin sauce, soy sauce, ginger, sriracha and vinegar.
5. Cook until the onions have softened, then stir in the water chestnuts and green onion and cook for another minute or so. Add salt and pepper to taste. Serve with lettuce leaves and eat by wrapping them up like a taco.

Nutrition:
Calories: : 157
Fat: 8 g
Cholesterol: 0 mg
Protein: : 15.7 g
Carbohydrates: : 10.5 g
Sugar: : 2.7 g
Fiber: 1.9 g

CRACKER BARREL'S FRIED MOZZARELLA

Preparation Time: 10 Minutes
Cooking Time: 10 Minutes
Servings: 4
Ingredients:

- 1-pound mozzarella or other cheese
- 2 eggs, beaten
- ¼ Cup water
- 11/2cups Italian breadcrumbs
- 1/2teaspoons garlic salt
- 1 Teaspoon Italian seasoning
- 2/3 cup flour
- 1/3 cup cornstarch

Directions:

1. Make thick cuts of the cheese. In a bowl, make an egg wash by beating together eggs and water. In another bowl, mix the breadcrumbs, garlic salt, and Italian seasoning. In a third bowl, mix together flour and cornstarch.
2. Heat vegetable oil in a frying pan.
3. Dip each piece of cheese into the flour, then egg wash, then breadcrumbs. Fry until golden brown. Remove from oil and drain on paper towel. Serve with marinara sauce.

Nutrition:
Calories: 682
Total Fat: 40 g
Cholesterol 79 mg
Sodium: 1,325 mg
Potassium 222mg
Total Carbohydrate 50g
Dietary fiber 3.8 g
Sugar: 3.4g
Protein: 32g

CINNAMON APPLES

Preparation Time: 10 minutes
Cooking time: 10 minutes
Servings: 3
Ingredients:
¼ cup butter
½ cup apple cider
1 tablespoon cornstarch
2 pounds Golden Delicious apples, cored, peeled and cut into wedges
1 teaspoon lemon juice
1 teaspoon cinnamon
⅛ teaspoon nutmeg
⅛ teaspoon allspice
¼ cup brown sugar
Directions:
In a large skillet, melt your butter over a medium to medium-low heat. Add the apples in a single layer, then top with the lemon juice followed by the brown sugar and spices.
Cover, reduce the heat to low, and allow the apples to simmer until tender.
Transfer the apples from the skillet to a serving bowl, leaving the juices in the skillet.
Whisk ½ cup of the juice together with the cornstarch in a small bowl. Turn the heat under the skillet up to medium-high and whisk the cornstarch mixture into the rest of the juices. Stir constantly until it thickens and there are no lumps.
Pour the juice over the bowl of apples and stir to coat.
Nutrition:
Calories 115
Protein 35
Carbs 26
Fat 5

LIMA BEANS

Preparation Time: 10 minutes
Cooking time: 30 minutes
Servings: 2
Ingredients:
1 cup water
1 chicken bouillon cube
2 slices bacon, chopped
1 clove garlic, peeled and lightly mashed
½ teaspoon red pepper flakes
½ teaspoon onion powder
1 teaspoon sugar
½ teaspoon black pepper
1 (1-pound) bag frozen lima beans
Directions:
Add the water and bouillon cube to a large pot and bring to a boil.
Stir in the remaining ingredients. Cover and turn the heat down so that the beans are simmering slightly.
Allow to simmer for 30 minutes, stirring occasionally. (Add more water if necessary.)
Remove the garlic and then, season with salt and pepper to taste.
Nutrition:
Calories 115
Protein 35
Carbs 26
Fat 5

GREEN BEANS

Preparation Time: 10 minutes
Cooking time: 35 minutes
Servings: 3
Ingredients:
4 slices thick-cut bacon, chopped into pieces
1 (14½-ounce) can cut green beans in water (do not drain)
½ cup onion, finely diced
1 teaspoon sugar
Salt
Pepper
Directions
Add the bacon to a large saucepan and cook over medium heat until it is browned but not yet crispy. Stir in the green beans (with liquid), onion and sugar. Bring to a boil, then reduce heat and simmer for 30–35 minutes.
Season to taste and serve.
Nutrition:
Calories 215
Protein 37
Carbs 26
Fat 5

CRACKER BARREL™ LOADED POTATO SALAD

Preparation Time 10 minutes
Cooking time 20 minutes
Servings 4
Ingredients:
Cooked potatoes (3 large)
Hardboiled eggs (3)
Minced onion (4 tbsp.)
Black pepper (as desired)
Dry mustard (1 tsp.)
Salt (1 tsp.)
The Saucepan:
Sugar (3 tsp.)
Eggs (2 uncooked)
Melted butter (3 tbsp.)
Hot vinegar (.5 cup)
Mayonnaise (1 cup)
Directions:
Mix the potatoes, eggs, onion, mustard, salt, and pepper.
Put the sugar, eggs, vinegar, and melted butter in a saucepan and simmer until thickened.
Combine with the mayonnaise and serve.
Nutrition: calories: 317 fat: 17.2g carbs: 33.9gprotein: 8.9gfiber: 6.5g

CRACKER BARREL™ AMBROSIA FRUIT SALAD

Preparation Time 10 minutes
Cooking time 0 minutes
Servings 4
Ingredients:
Pineapple chunks (1 can)
Oranges (6 peeled and cut into chunks)
Coconut (.25 lb.)
Apples (2 chopped)
Sugar to garnish
Directions:
Prepare the salad using alternate layers to your liking.
Serve cold.
Nutrition: Calories: 577 Cal Fats: 55.1g Carbs: 4.7g Protein: 19g Fiber: 1.6g

CRACKER BARREL SAWMILL GRAVY COPYCAT

Preparation time: 20 minutes
Cooking time: 30 minutes
Serving: 6
Ingredients
1/4 cup fried meat grease
One sausage patty; cooked and crumbled
1/4 cup bacon bits
1/4 cup allpurpose flour
2 cups of milk
salt according to your taste
coarsely ground black pepper; to taste
Directions:
Take fat off after frying the bacon, ham or chicken and weigh 1/4 cup drippings.
Return to saucepan and add flour. Stir until combined.
Then you put the milk and cook over medium heat, continually stirring until thick and bubbling.
Season with salt and coarsely ground pepper to taste.
Stir in crumbled bits of sausage and bacon. Stir and serve well.
 Nutrition: calories 340, fat 8, fiber 2, carbs 8, protein 6

COPYCAT CRACKER BARREL SPROUTS AND KALE SALAD

Preparation Time 10 minutes
Cooking time 20 minutes
Servings 6
Ingredients
1 bunch of kale
1 pound of Brussels sprouts
16 ounces. Bag Craisins
8 ounces. chopped pecans
Maple Vinaigrette
1/2 c. olive oil
1/4 c. Apple Cider Vinegar
4 Tbs. maple syrup
1 teaspoon. dry mustard
Directions:
Sprinkle or thinly slice the kale and Brussel and installed a salad bowl.
Toast pecans for 60ninety seconds in a skillet over high heat.
Bowl with pecans and craisins.
Mix well all the elements of the vinaigrette.
Pour over salad vinaigrette and mix to cowl evenly. Let at least four hours or overnight stay within the fridge.
Nutrition: Calories 290, Carbs 49 g, Fats 6 g, Protein 9 g

CRACKER BARREL'S CLAMS BRUSCHETTA

Preparation Time: 15 minutes
Cooking Time: 2 minutes
Servings: 8
Ingredients:

- 8 slices Italian bread
- 1 clove garlic, halved 1/2cup extra virgin olive oil
- 1 cup (or 2 6-ounce cans) chopped clam meat, drained
- 4 ripe tomatoes, cut into slices
- Salt and freshly ground pepper to taste
- 12 fresh arugula or basil leaves, rinsed and dried

Directions:

1. Preheat grill, then toast both sides of the bread slices.
2. Rub the garlic onto each side of the bread to infuse with flavor.
3. Place a tomato slice and some clam meat on each bread slice. Sprinkle with salt and pepper to taste. Drizzle olive oil on top.
4. Cut arugula or basil thinly and place onto bruschetta. Serve.

Nutrition:
Calories: : 424.4.
Total Fat: 29.4 g
Cholesterol 19.3 mg
Sodium: 276.8 mg
Total Carbohydrate 29.1 g
Dietary Fiber 3.4 g
Sugar: : 5.2 g
Protein: 12.6g

MACARONI AND CHEESE

Preparation Time: 10 minutes
Cooking time: 30 minutes
Servings: 3
Ingredients:
2 tablespoons butter
2 tablespoons flour
1 teaspoon salt
1 teaspoon dry mustard
2½ cups milk
½ pound (about 2 cups) cheddar (divided)
½ pound (2 cups) elbow macaroni, cooked
Directions:
Preheat the oven to 375°F.
Melt the butter in a saucepan, then stir in the flour, salt, and mustard.
Whisk in the milk and stir constantly until the sauce begins to thicken.
Stir in 1½ cups of the cheese. Continue to stir until melted, then remove from the heat.
Add the cooked elbow macaroni and the cheese sauce to a buttered casserole dish. Stir until the macaroni is covered with sauce. Top with the remaining cheese and bake for 25 minutes or until the top is browned and the cheese is bubbly.
Nutrition:
Calories 115
Protein 35
Carbs 26
Fat 5

CRACKER BARREL HASH BROWN CASSEROLE

Preparation time: 20 minutes
Cooking time: 40 minutes
Serving: 6
Ingredients:
1 pound frozen hash browns
¼ cup margarine
1 (10ounce) can cream of chicken soup
½ pint sour cream
¼ cup peeled and chopped onion
1 cup grated Cheddar cheese
½ teaspoon salt
1/8 teaspoon pepper
Directions:
Preheat oven to 350°F.
Spray a large baking dish with cooking spray.
Mix all the **ingredients** in a bowl.
Place combined **ingredients** into the baking dish.
Bake until brown on top.
Nutrition: 320.7 calories; 7.9 g protein; 20.9 g carbohydrates; 60.6 mg cholesterol; 626.6 mg sodium.

CHAPTER 3

SOUPS

CRACKER BARREL CHICKEN AND DUMPLINGS SOUP

Preparation Time: 20 Minutes
Cooking Time: 35 minutes
Servings: 4
Ingredients:

- 2 cups all-purpose flour
- ½ tsp. baking powder
- Salt to taste
- 2 tbsp. butter
- 1 cup milk
- 2 cans of chicken broth
- 3 Cups chicken, cooked

Directions:

1. The flour, baking powder, and salt are mixed in a dish. Cut the butter with a fork or pastry blender to dry **ingredients**. Stir in the milk until the dough forms a ball, mixing with a fork.
2. A work surface thickly flourishes. You will need a rolling pin to cut the dumplings with and something. I like using a cutter on pizza. I like using a little spatula, too, to lift the dumplings off the cutting board.
3. With a rolling pin roll the dough thin out. Dip your cutter into the flour, and cut the dumplings into tiny squares. To them, it's all right not to be perfect. Only eye the bone. Some will be bigger, some smaller, and some could be funny in shape.
4. Put them on a heavily floured plate using the floured spatula. Just keep floating in between the dumpling's layers.
5. Carry the broth to a boil to cook them. Drop the dumplings in one at a time and stir while adding them. The extra flour on them helps the broth thicken.
6. Cook them for about 20 Minutes or until they taste no doughy.
7. Add the chicken to the saucepan and serve.

Nutrition:
Calories: : 286 Fat: 44.1g
Carbs: 31. 7g Protein: : 32.3g
Sodium: : 324mg

CHICKEN & DUMPLINGS SOUP FROM CRACKER BARREL COPYCAT

Preparation Time10 minutes **Cooking time** 45 minutes **Servings** 5
Ingredients
1/2 teaspoon salt
1 broiler/fryer chicken (about 3 pounds), cut up
2 celery ribs, chopped
2 bay leaves
1 large onion, chopped
3/4 cup allpurpose flour, divided
3 garlic cloves, minced
2 tablespoons canola oil
1/2 cup white wine or apple cider
6 cups chicken stock
1/2 teaspoon freshly ground pepper
2 medium carrots, chopped
2 teaspoons sugar
5 whole peppercorns
DUMPLINGS:
2 teaspoons baking powder
11/3 cups allpurpose flour
3/4 teaspoon salt
1 tablespoon butter, melted
2/3 cup 2% milk
SOUP:
2 teaspoons minced fresh thyme
Additional salt and pepper to taste
2 teaspoons minced fresh parsley
1/2 cup heavy whipping cream

Directions:

Blend 1/2 cup rice, salt and pepper in a shallow bowl. Add one piece of chicken at a time and toss to coat; shake off excess. Within 6qt. Heat the oil over medium to high heat, stockpot. Brown chicken all sides in batches; remove from pan.

In the same pan, add the onion, carrots and celery; cook and stir for 68 minutes or until the onion is tender. Add garlic; stir and cook for 1 minute. Add 1/4 cup flour until mixed. Gradually add in stock, continuously stirring. Stir in wine, sugar, leaves from the bay and peppercorns. Return the chicken to saucepan; bring it to a boil. Reduce heat; cook, cover, for 2025 minutes, or until juices from chicken run clear.

For dumplings, whisk flour, baking powder and salt in a cup. Whisk the milk and the melted butter in another bowl until combined. Add mixture to flour; stir until moistened (do not overmix). Drop onto a parchmentlined baking sheet by rounded tablespoonful; set aside.

Remove the chicken from stockpot; slightly cool off. Dispose of bay leaves and skim soup fat. Remove from the chicken skin and bones, and discard. Use 2 forks, slice meat coarsely into 1to 11/2in. Pieces; get back to broth. Cook on warm, sealed, until the mixture reaches a simmer.

Drop the dumplings on top of the soup to simmer, a few at a time. Reduce heat to low; cook, cover, for 1518 minutes or until clean comes out a toothpick inserted in the center of the dumplings (do not lift the cover while simmering). Stir gently in cream, parsley and thyme. Season with salt and pepper to taste.

Nutrition: Calories: 179 Fat: 15.7g. Carbs: 4.8g. Protein: 5.6g. Fiber: 0.8g.

CRACKER BARREL SOUP

Preparation Time15 minutes
Cooking time 10 minutes
Servings 4
Ingredients
1⁄2 lb hash browns
1/8 cup margarine or 1/8 cup spread, dissolved
1 (2 1/16 ounce) can cream of chicken soup
1⁄4 16 ounces sharp cream
1⁄8 cup onion, stripped and hacked
1⁄2 cup cheddar, ground
1⁄4 teaspoon salt
1/16 teaspoon pepper
Directions:
Preheat stove to 350°F and splash a 11 x 14 preparing dish with salted butter.
Combine the above fixings, place in arranged dish and cook for 45 minutes or until earthy colored on top.
Nutrition: calories 185, fat 4, fiber 5.4, carbs 6.4, protein 7

PANERA BROCCOLI CHEDDAR SOUP

Preparation Time: 10 Minutes
Cooking Time: 20 Minutes
Servings: 4
Ingredients:

- ½ stick butter
- ½ yellow onion, diced
- 2 cloves garlic
- 3 Cups chicken broth
- 2 tbsp. flour
- 1/4 tsp. nutmeg
- 1/4 cup carrots
- 4 cups broccoli florets
- 2 ½ cups cheddar cheese
- Salt to taste
- Pepper to taste

Directions:

1. Raising the cheese and letting it reach room temperature.
2. Melt the butter over medium heat in a big pot oven.
3. Add the onions and heat for about 5 minutes, until soft and translucent.
4. Add the garlic, and cook for an extra minute.
5. Add one Tablespoon of flour and mix to blend. Warm-up for one minute, stirring continuously.
6. Garnish the chicken broth slowly and mix to combine. The nutmeg is added.
7. Add half and half, slightly increase the heat to bring the mixture to a light bubble, and allow it to thicken around 5 minutes.
8. Reduce to medium heat. Add the broccoli and carrots and let the mixture simmer until very tender. Occasionally shake as served.
9. Turn off the heat and put the pot into a cool burner. Enable 5 Minutes for the foundation to cool down.
10. Sprinkle over the shredded cheese over the remaining 1 Tablespoon of flour.
11. In 4 separate lots, add the cheese/flour, stirring to mix as each load is applied.
12. Once the cheese is melted, serve it straight away and enjoy it!

Nutrition:
Calories: : 198
Fat: 5.9g
Carbs: 17. 6g
Protein: : 5.8g
Sodium: : 354mg

CHAPTER 4

POULTRY AND FISH

CRACKER BARREL CORNFLAKE CRUSTED CHICKEN
Preparation Time: 10 minutes
Cooking time: 45 minutes
Servings: 4
Ingredients:

- 4 boneless skinless chicken breasts, cut into large strips
- 3 Cups cornflakes
- 2 Tablespoons melted butter
- 1 large egg, beaten
- 1 Teaspoon water
- Salt
- Pepper
- Chicken poultry seasoning

Directions:

1. Preheat the oven to 400°F.
2. Lay out the chicken breasts and season both sides with salt, pepper, and poultry seasoning.
3. In a shallow dish, combine the water and egg.
4. In a separate shallow dish, crush the cornflakes and season with some more poultry seasoning.
5. Dip each breast in the egg mixture, then roll it in the cornflakes.
6. Place the chicken on a baking sheet and pat more cornflakes on top.
7. Bake for about 30–35 minutes or until the chicken is done.

Nutrition:
Calories: : 121
Total Fat: 23g
Carbs: 12g
Protein: : 81g
Fiber: 0g

CRACKER BARREL HONEY GRILLED SALMON

Preparation Time: 10 minutes

Cooking time 30 minutes

Servings 4

Ingredients

- 1/4cup of honey
- 1/3 cup of soy sauce
- 1/4cup of dark brown sugar, packed
- 1/4cup of pineapple juice
- 2 tablespoons fresh lemon juice
- 1 tablespoon apple cider vinegar
- 1 tablespoon olive oil
- 1 teaspoon ground black pepper, plus more for seasoning the salmon
- 1/2teaspoon cayenne pepper
- 1/2teaspoon paprika
- 1/2teaspoon garlic powder
- 4 (8 ounces) salmon fillets
- Rice and vegetables, to serve

Directions

1. In a medium saucepan over medium-low heat, combine all the **ingredients** except the fish. Bring it to a boil, then reduce the warmth, occasionally stirring until the sauce thickens to the consistency of syrup.

2. Cook the salmon to your preference, either on the grill or in the oven.

3. Serve the salmon with sauce over the highest, with rice and vegetables.

Nutrition:
Calories: 233
Total Fat: 14g
Carbs: 36g
Protein: 44g
Fiber: 0g

CRACKER BARREL'S GREEN CHILI JACK CHICKEN

Preparation Time 10 minutes
Cooking time 45 minutes
Servings 4
Ingredients
1 pound chicken strips
1 teaspoon chili powder
4 ounces green chilies
2 cups Monterey Jack cheese, shredded
¼ cup salsa
Directions
Sprinkle the chicken with the chili powder while heating some oil over medium heat.
Cook the chicken strips until they are half cooked, and then place the green chilies on top of the chicken. Lower the heat to low.
Cook for 1 to 2 minutes before adding the cheese on top. Keep cooking the chicken and cheese until the cheese melts.
Serve the chicken with the salsa.
Nutrition: Calories 516, Total Fat 24.4 g, Carbs 8.5 g, Protein 64.2 g

CRACKER BARREL INSPIRED BROCCOLI CHEDDAR CHICKEN CASSEROLE

Preparation Time 10 minutes
Cooking time 45 minutes
Servings 4
Ingredients
4 boneless skinless chicken breasts
Kosher salt
Freshly ground black pepper
1 c. whole milk
1 (10.5oz.) can cheddar cheese soup
1/2 tsp. paprika
1 c. shredded sharp cheddar
1 (10oz.) bag frozen broccoli florets
1 c. crushed Ritz crackers, divided
Directions:
Preheat oven to 350°. Pat each chicken breast dry using paper towels. Season with salt and pepper and place in a large ovenproof casserole dish.
In a large mixing bowl, combine milk, soup, paprika, and cheddar, then fold in broccoli and half the crackers. Pour over chicken, covering entirely.
Top with remaining crackers and bake until chicken is fully cooked, 45 minutes.
Nutrition: Calories: 220 Protein: 3g Fat: 1g Carbs: 56g

CRACKER BARREL GRILLED CHICKEN TENDERS

Preparation time: 5 minutes
Cooking Time: 45 minutes
Servings: 4
Ingredients

2 teaspoons lime juice, freshly squeezed
1 pound cut chicken breasts or chicken tenders
2 tablespoons honey
½ cup Italian dressing
Directions

Place the chicken tenderloins with wet ingredients into a large plastic bag. Let marinate in a refrigerator for an hour.

Add the chicken & liquid to a large skillet. Cook until the liquid is reduced & chicken turns golden, but not dry, over medium heat. Ensure that you turn the chicken pieces a couple of times during the cooking

Nutrition: Calories: 3.6 Protein: 0.2 Grams Fat: 0 Grams Carbs: 0.8 Grams

CRACKER BARREL'S APPLE WALNUT CHICKEN SALAD
Preparation Time: 10 minutes plus 3 hours brining time **Cooking time** 8 minutes **Servings** 2–4
Ingredients
For the chicken
- 3 cups of water
- 1 tablespoon of salt
- 1/2teaspoon of garlic powder
- 1/4teaspoon of hickory-flavored liquid smoke
- 1 boneless chicken breast, pounded to a ½-inch thickness
- 1/2teaspoon of ground black pepper
- 1 tablespoon of oil

For the balsamic vinaigrette:
- 1/4cup of red wine vinegar
- 3 tablespoons of granulated sugar
- 3 tablespoons of honey
- 1 tablespoon of Dijon mustard
- 1/2teaspoon of salt
- 1 teaspoon of minced garlic
- 1 teaspoon of lemon juice
- 1/2teaspoon of Italian seasoning
- 1/4teaspoon of dried tarragon
- 1 Pinch of ground black pepper
- 1 cup of extra-virgin olive oil

For the candied walnuts:
- 1 teaspoon of peanut oil
- 1 teaspoon of honey
- 2 tablespoons of granulated sugar
- 1/4teaspoon of vanilla extract
- 1/8teaspoon of salt
- A pinch of cayenne pepper
- 3/4 cup of chopped walnuts

For the salad:
- 4 cups of romaine lettuce, chopped
- 4 cups of red leaf lettuce, chopped
- 1 apple, diced
- 1/2small red onion, sliced
- 1/2cup of diced celery
- 1/4cup of blue cheese, crumbled

Directions:
1. For the chicken brine:
2. Mix the water, salt, garlic powder, and liquid smoke in a medium-sized bowl.
3. Add the chicken, cover, and refrigerate for a minimum of three hours.
4. For the balsamic vinaigrette
5. Whisk together all ingredients listed EXCEPT the oil.
6. Gradually pour in the oil while whisking. Refrigerate until able to serve.
7. For the candied walnuts
8. In a skillet, mix the groundnut oil, honey, sugar, vanilla, salt, and cayenne pepper, and cook over medium heat.
9. When the mixture starts to boil, add the walnuts and stir until the sugar begins to caramelize. Stir for 1 minute then pour onto a baking sheet covered with paper. Allow the nuts to chill.
10. For the salad:
11. Remove the chicken from the brine and pat it dry with a towel and season with black pepper.
12. Place the chicken on a hot grill. Grill for 3 to 4 minutes on all sides or until cooked through and juices run clear. Let it cool and slice it into strips.
13. In a salad bowl, combine the romaine lettuce, red leaf lettuce, apple, onion, celery, and bleu. Divide it onto plates and pour on some dressing. Top with sliced chicken and candied walnuts.
14. Refrigerate any unused dressing.

Nutrition:
Calories: 201.6
Total Fat: 20.6g
Carbs: 3.6g
Protein: 22.6g
Fiber: 5.3g

APPLE CHEDDAR CHICKEN

Preparation Time 20 minutes
Cooking time 30 minutes
Servings 68
Ingredients:
5 cooked skinless hen breast s, entire or cubed (Cracker Barrel makes use of the whole breast, but both choices work.)
2 cans of apple pie filling with a cut of apples in 1/3 1 bag extrasharp cheddar cheese
1 row Ritz crackers, beaten 1 cup melted butter
Directions:
Preheat the oven to 350°F.
Combine the chicken, apple pie filling, and cheddar cheese in a mixing bowl. Stir together.
Pour the mixture into a greased casserole dish.
Mix Ritz crackers with the melted butter. Spread over the casserole.
Bake for 45 minutes or till it starts evolved to bubble.
Nutrition: calories 125, fat 9, fiber 2, carbs 8, protein 6

CRACKER BARREL CHICKEN AND DUMPLINGS

Preparation Time: 1 hour
Cooking Time: 2 hours **Servings**: 6
Ingredients:
1 whole chicken
2 quarts water
2 teaspoons salt
½ teaspoon pepper
2 cups allpurpose flour
½ teaspoon baking soda
½ teaspoon salt
3 tablespoons shortening
¾ cup buttermilk
Directions:
In a heavy bottomed pot, boil chicken in water mixed with salt. Cover, then lower heat. Simmer for about 1 hour or until tender enough that the meat almost falls off the bone.
Using a slotted spoon, transfer chicken to a plate and cool. Then, remove bones and chop into small pieces.
In same pot, add broth and bring to a boil Add pepper.
In a bowl, mix flour, baking soda, and salt. Fold in shortening. Pour in buttermilk and mix everything until incorporated.
Knead dough 4 to 5 times. Pinch off about ½ inche size balls of dough and to the boiling broth. Reduce heat to mediumlow. Simmer for about 8 to 10 minutes while stirring every now and then. Add chicken to pot and stir. Serve immediately.
Nutrition: Calories: 711, Fat: 41 g, Saturated fat: 12 g, Carbs: 33 g, Sugar: 2 g, Fibers: 1 g, Protein: 48 g

CRACKER BARREL CHICKEN POTPIE

Preparation Time 30 minutes
Cooking time 40 minutes
Servings 5
Ingredients
Two tablespoons canola oil
One medium onion, choppe d
1/2 cup allpurpose flour
One teaspoon poultry seasoning
3/4 cup 2% milk
One can (141/2 ounces) chicken broth
3 cups cubed cooked chicken
2 cups of frozen mixed vegetables, thawed
One sheet refrigerated pie crust
Directions:
Oven preheat to 450 ° C. Heat oil in a large saucepan over mediumhigh heat. Add onion; stir and cook until tender. Season with flour and poultry until blended; whisk slowly in broth and milk. Bring to a boil and stir continuously; cook and stir for 23 minutes or until thickened. Stir in vegetables and chicken.
Shift to 9in grained deepsoaked pie plate; place the crust over the filling. Trim, seal, and the edges of the flute. In crust split slits. Bake for 1520 minutes or until golden brown is cooked, and bubbly fill.
Nutrition: Calories 131, Fat 1, Fiber 3, Carbs 5, Protein 3

CRACKER BARREL CHICKEN FRIED CHICKEN
Preparation Time: 10 minutes
Cooking time: 30 minutes Servings: 4
Ingredients:
Chicken

- 1/2cup all-purpose flour
- 1 Teaspoon poultry seasoning
- ½ Teaspoon salt
- ½ Teaspoon pepper
- 1 egg, slightly beaten
- 1 tablespoon water
- 4 boneless skinless chicken breasts, pounded to a ½-inch thickness
- 1 cup vegetable oil

Gravy

- 2 Tablespoons all-purpose flour
- ¼ Teaspoon salt
- ¼ Teaspoon pepper
- 11/4cups milk

Directions:
1. Preheat the oven to 200°F.
2. In a shallow dish, combine the flour, poultry seasoning, salt, and pepper.
3. In another shallow dish, mix the beaten egg and water.
4. First, dip both sides of the chicken breasts in the flour mixture, then dip them in the egg mixture, and then back into the flour mixture.
5. Heat the vegetable oil over medium-high heat in a large deep skillet. A cast iron is a good choice if you have one. Add the chicken and cook for about 15 minutes, or until fully cooked, turning over about halfway through.
6. Transfer the chicken to a cookie sheet and place in the oven to maintain temperature.
7. Remove all but 2 Tablespoons of oil from the skillet you cooked the chicken in.
8. Prepare the gravy by whisking the dry gravy **ingredients** together in a bowl. Then whisk them into the oil in the skillet, stirring thoroughly to remove lumps. When the flour begins to brown, slowly whisk in the milk. Continue cooking and whisking for about 2 minutes or until the mixture thickens.
9. Top chicken with some of the gravy.

Nutrition:
Calories: : 281
Total Fat: 30g
Carbs: 2g
Protein: : 71g
Fiber: 0g

CRACKER BARREL SUNDAY CHICKEN
Preparation Time: 10 minutes
Cooking time: 10 minutes
Servings: 4
Ingredients:

- Oil for frying
- 4 boneless, skinless chicken breasts
- 1 cups all-purpose flour
- 1 cup bread crumbs
- 2 Teaspoons salt
- 2 Teaspoons black pepper
- 1 cup buttermilk
- 1/2cup water

Directions:

1. Add 3–4 inches of oil to a large pot or a deep fryer and preheat to 350°F.
2. Mix the flour, breadcrumbs, salt, and pepper in a shallow dish. To a separate shallow dish, add the buttermilk and water; stir.
3. Pound the chicken breasts to a consistent size. Dry them with a paper towel, then sprinkle with salt and pepper.
4. Dip the seasoned breasts in the flour mixture, then the buttermilk mixture, then back into the flour.
5. Add the breaded chicken to the hot oil and fry for about 8 minutes. Turn the chicken as necessary so that it cooks evenly on both sides.
6. Remove the chicken to either a wire rack or a plate lined with paper towels to drain.
7. Serve with mashed potatoes or whatever sides you love.

Nutrition:
Calories: : 681
Total Fat: 30g
Carbs: 3g
Protein: : 71g
Fiber: 0g

CRACKER BARREL CHICKEN POT PIE
Preparation Time: 30 minutes Cooking time: 45 minutes Servings: 4
Ingredients:

- 1/2cup butter
- 1 medium onion, diced
- 1 (14.5-ounce) can chicken broth
- 1 cup half and half milk
- 1/2cup all-purpose flour
- 1 carrot, diced
- 1 celery stalk, diced
- 3 medium potatoes, peeled and diced
- 3 Cups cooked chicken, diced
- 1/2cup frozen peas
- 1 Teaspoon chicken seasoning
- ½ Teaspoon salt
- ½ Teaspoon ground pepper
- 1 single refrigerated pie crust
- 1 Egg
- Water

Directions:

1. Preheat the oven to 375°F. In a large skillet, heat the butter over medium heat, add the leeks and sauté for 3 minutes. Sprinkle flour over the mixture, and continue to stir constantly for 3 minutes. Whisking constantly, blend in the chicken broth and milk. Bring the mixture to a boil. Reduce heat to medium-low.
2. Add the carrots, celery, potatoes, salt, pepper, and stir to combine. Cook for 10-15 minutes or until veggies are cooked through but still crisp. Add chicken and peas. Stir to combine.
3. Transfer chicken filling to a deep 9-inch pie dish.
4. Fit the pie crust sheet on top and press the edges around the dish to seal the crust. Trim the excess if needed.
5. In a separate bowl, whisk an egg with 1 tablespoon of water, and brush the mixture over the top of the pie. With a knife, cut a few slits to let steam escape.
6. Bake the pie in the oven on the middle oven rack 20 to 30 minutes until the crust becomes golden brown. Let the pie rest for about 15 minutes before serving.

Note: Alternatively to serve it like exactly Cracker Barrel, use individual baking dishes and proceed the same way, using homemade or store-bought crust that you can roll out will make it easier to shape the required crust for each dish.

Nutrition:
Calories: : 111 Total Fat: 23g Carbs: 12g Protein: : 81g
Fiber: 0g

CRACKER BARREL SHRIMP BROCCOLI CAVATAPPI

Preparation Time: 10 minutes

Cooking time 15 minutes **Servings** 4-6 *Ingredients*

- 1-pound shrimp, peeled and deveined
- 2 cups dried cavatappi pasta
- 2 cups of broccoli florets
- 1 tablespoon butter
- 2 cloves garlic, minced
- 2 tablespoons of flour
- 1 1/3 cups of milk
- 1 1/4cups of Parmesan cheese, freshly grated, divided
- 2 tablespoons of cream cheese
- 1/4teaspoon salt
- Freshly ground black pepper to taste

Directions

1. Cook the shrimp, either on a hot grill (which will add that wonderful smoky flavor) or just fry them in a skillet. Either way, cook them for about 2–3 minutes on all sides, just until they turn pink. Keep warm after they need finishing cooking.

2. Cook the pasta in a pot of boiling water until its tender. Everyone likes pasta in a particular way, so cook to your preference. Steam the broccoli.

3. In a large saucepan, melt the butter over medium heat. Add the garlic and cook until fragrant, about 1 minute.

4. Stir in the flour and gradually whisk in the milk. Continue cooking for about 5 minutes, or until it thickens. Add 1 cup of the Parmesan cheese and, therefore, the cheese, and season with salt and pepper. Whisk together until the cheese is melted, and consequently, the mixture is smooth.

5. Add in the cooked pasta and broccoli and stir to make sure everything is coated. Serve plated pasta and broccoli with shrimp on the highest. Add extra Parmesan if you desire.

Nutrition:
Calories: 520
Total Fat: 22g
Carbs: 33g
Protein: 49g
Fiber: 7g

CHAPTER 5

BEEF AND PORK

GRILLED PORK CHOPS

 Preparation Time: 20 minutes
Cooking Time: 10 minutes
Servings: 4
Ingredients:

- 1/4 cup kosher salt
- 1/4 cup sugar
- 2 cups water
- 2 cups ice water
- 4 center-cut pork rib chops (1 inch thick and 8 ounces each)
- 2 tablespoons canola oil
- Basic Rub:
- 3 tablespoons paprika
- 1 teaspoon each garlic powder, onion powder, ground cumin and ground mustard
- 1 teaspoon coarsely ground pepper
- 1/2 teaspoon ground chipotle pepper

Directions:
1. In a large saucepan, combine salt, sugar and 2 cups water; cook and stir over medium heat until salt and sugar are dissolved. Remove from heat. Add 2 cups ice water to cool brine to room temperature. Place pork chops in a large resealable plastic bag; add cooled brine.
2. Seal bag, pressing out as much air as possible; turn to coat chops. Place in a 13x9-in. baking dish. Refrigerate 8-12 hours. Remove chops from brine, rinse, and pat dry. Discard brine. Brush both sides of chops with oil. In a small bowl, mix rub **ingredients**; rub over pork chops. Let stand at room temperature 30 minutes. Grill chops on an oiled rack, covered, over medium heat 4-6 minutes on each side or until a thermometer reads 145°. Let stand 5 minutes before serving.

Nutrition:
Calories: 300,
Fat: 18g,
Cholesterol: 72mg,
Sodium: 130mg,
Carbohydrate: 5g,
Protein: 30g

CRACKER BARREL'S TUSCAN BUTTER BURGER

Preparation Time: 15 minutes
Cooking Time: 30 minutes
Servings: 4
Ingredients
For the Chicken Burgers

- 1 cup panko
- 1 ½ pounds ground chicken
- 4 green onions, minced
- 2 tablespoon extra-virgin olive oil
- 1 teaspoon Himalayan pink salt, black pepper, garlic blend

For the Tuscan Butter Sauce

- ¼ cup Parmesan, finely grated
- 2 tablespoon butter
- ½ cup heavy cream
- 1 tablespoon tomato paste
- ¼ teaspoon Himalayan pink salt, black pepper, garlic blend

For Assembly

- 4 seeded hamburger buns, split & lightly toasted
- 1 cup large basil leaves, fresh
- 1 jar oil-packed sun-dried tomatoes (7-ounces), drained

Directions

1. For Chicken Burgers: Combine the chicken together with panko, green onions & 1 teaspoon Himalayan pink salt, garlic blend, black pepper in a medium bowl.
2. Cook oil over medium-high heat in a large skillet. Form 4 even-sized patties from the chicken mixture using slightly dampened hands, placing the patties carefully into the hot skillet. Cook for 8 to 10 minutes, until turn golden, flipping once during the **cooking time**. Remove the patties to a large plate; drain any excess oil.
3. For Tuscan butter Sauce: Place the skillet over medium-low heat & add butter & tomato paste. Cook for a minute, whisking frequently. Whisk in the Parmesan, heavy cream & ¼ teaspoon Himalayan pink salt, black pepper, garlic blend. Bring the mixture to a simmer. Once done; decrease the heat to low & let simmer until parmesan is melted & the sauce is reduced slightly, for a couple of more minutes. Remove from the heat.
4. Place the burger patties on the bottom buns. Spoon the Tuscan butter sauce on top of patties and then top with sun-dried tomatoes and basil. Close the sandwich with top bun.

Nutrition:
897 calories
60g total fats
40g protein

SOUTHWEST STEAK
Preparation Time: 20 Minutes
Cooking time: 10 Minutes
Servings: 2
Ingredients:

- 2 (6-ounce) sirloin steaks, or your favorite cut
- 2 Teaspoons blackened steak seasoning
- 1/2cup red peppers, sliced
- 1/2cup green peppers, sliced
- 2 Tablespoons unsalted butter
- 1 cup yellow onion, sliced
- 2 cloves garlic, minced
- Salt, to taste
- Pepper, to taste
- 2 slices cheddar cheese
- 2 slices Monterey jack cheese
- Vegetable medley or/and garlic mashed potatoes, for serving

Directions:

1. Preheat a cast iron (or another heavy skillet) or a grill.
2. Season the meat with steak seasoning and cook to your desired doneness (about 3–4 minutes on each side for medium-rare).
3. In another skillet, melt the butter and cook the peppers, onion, and garlic. Season with salt and pepper.
4. Just before the steak has reached your desired doneness, top with a slice of each cheese and cook a bit longer until the cheese melts.
5. Serve the steaks with pepper and onion mix and garlic mashed potatoes.

Nutrition:
Calories: : 350
Total Fat: 17g
Carbs: 34g
Protein: : 14g
Fiber: 2g

BOURBON STREET STEAK

Preparation Time: 10 Minutes   **Cooking time: 20 Minutes Servings: 4**
Ingredients:
Steak **ingredients**

- 4 New York strip steaks, 1-inch thick
- 6 tablespoons Worcestershire sauce
- 5 tablespoons soy sauce
- ¼ Cup apple cider vinegar
- 1 1/2tablespoons chili powder
- 1 1/2tablespoons garlic, minced
- 4 teaspoons meat tenderizer
- 2 Tablespoons smoked paprika (regular paprika is also fine)
- 1 1/2tablespoons black pepper
- 2 Teaspoons cayenne pepper
- 2 Teaspoons onion salt
- 1 Teaspoon dried oregano
- 1-quart beef stock

Other **ingredients**

- 1 tablespoon butter
- 1 onion, sliced
- 1 1/2cups sliced mushrooms
- 2 garlic cloves, minced
- 4 large potatoes, cut into 1-inch cubes
- Oil for deep frying

Directions:

1. In a large resalable bag or container with a lid, combine all the **ingredients** and mix to make sure they are well combined, and the steak is covered. Refrigerate for at least 8 hours or overnight, turning from time to time. If you have a deep fryer, turn it on so the oil is ready to fry the potatoes. Otherwise, in a sauce pot, heat the frying oil so it reaches 350-degree F.
2. Preheat the grill, broiler, or skillet. Cook the steaks to your preference, about 4 minutes per side for medium. Transfer to a plate and keep warm with foil.
3. While steaks are cooking, in a large skillet, melt the butter over medium heat. Add the onions and sauté for 2 minutes. Add the mushrooms and sauté until mushrooms are golden, about 4-5 minutes.
4. Simultaneously, deep fry the potatoes until tender and golden brown, about 6-8 minutes. Remove from oil onto a plate or basket lined with paper towel absorb excess oil. Season with salt, and paprika, if desired.
5. Serve steaks top with mushrooms and onions and a side of potatoes.

Nutrition:
Calories: : 400 Total Fat: 19g Carbs: 39g Protein: : 16g Fiber: 2g

OUTBACK STYLE STEAK
Preparation Time: 40 minutes
Cooking time: 10 minutes
Servings: 4
Ingredients:

- 4 (6-ounce) sirloin or ribeye steaks
- 2 Tablespoons olive oil
- 2 Tablespoons Old Bay Seasoning
- 2 Tablespoons brown sugar
- 1 Teaspoon garlic powder
- 1 Teaspoon salt
- ½ Teaspoon black pepper
- ½ Teaspoon onion powder
- ½ Teaspoon ground cumin

Directions:

1. Take the steaks out of the fridge and let them sit at room temperature for about 20 minutes.
2. Combine all the seasonings and mix well.
3. Rub the steaks with oil and some of the spice mixture, covering all the surfaces. Let the steaks sit for 20–30 minutes.
4. Meanwhile, heat your grill to medium-high.
5. Cook the steaks for about 5 Minutes on each side for medium rare (or to an internal temperature of 130°F.) Let them sit for 5 Minutes before serving.

Nutrition:
Calories: : 254
Total Fat: 13g
Carbs: 56g
Protein: : 45g
Fiber: 3g

CRACKER BARREL'S GREEN BEANS WITH BACON

Preparation Time: 10 minutes
Cooking Time: 45 minutes
Servings: 6
Ingredients
¼ pound sliced bacon, cut into 1inch piec es
3 cans (14.5 ounces each) green beans, with liquid
¼ yellow onion, peeled, chopped
1 teaspoon granulated sugar
½ teaspoon salt
½ teaspoon fresh ground black pepper
Directions
Halfcook the bacon in a saucepan—make sure it does not get crispy.
Add the green beans with the liquid to the browned bacon and season with salt, pepper, and sugar.
Top the green beans with the onion and then cover the pan until the mixture boils.
Lower the heat and allow the mixture to simmer for another 45 minutes before serving.
Nutrition: Calories 155.3, Total Fat 9 g, Carbs 15.7 g, Protein 6 g

CRACKER BARREL BEEF STEW

Preparation time: 10 minutes **Cooking time**: 20 minutes Serving: 6
Ingredients:
1 pound stewing beef, cut into bitesize pieces
1 medium white onion, peeled, chopped
2 large turnips, peeled, cut into bitesize pieces
1 cup frozen peas
4 medium potatoes, peeled, cut into bitesize pieces
5 carrots, peeled, cut into bitesize pieces
1 ½ teaspoon salt
½ cup allpurpose flour
¾ teaspoon ground black pepper
¼ teaspoon dried thyme
3 tablespoons olive oil, divided
¼ cup ketchup
4 cups beef broth
Directions: :
Take a large bowl, place beef pieces in it, season with salt and black pepper, add flour and then toss until mixed. Pour 2 tablespoons of olive oil in a large pot, heat it over mediumhigh heat until hot, add beef pieces and then cook until brown on all sides.
Transfer beef pieces to a plate, add remaining oil into the pot and when hot, add onion and cook for 5 minutes until golden brown. Add carrot, turnip and potato pieces in it, return beef pieces in it, add ketchup and thyme, pour in the broth. Stir until combined and then simmer the stew over low heat level for 1 hour and 30 minutes until thoroughly cooked, cover the pot with its lid. Then add peas, cook for 5 minutes until hot and then serve.
Nutrition Information per Serving: 543 Cal; 17 g Fat; 59 g Carbohydrates; 10 g Fiber; 14 g Sugars; 40 g Protein 4

CRACKER BARREL HAM AND RED EYE GRAVY

Preparation time: 10 minutes
Cooking time: 20 minutes
Serving: 2
Ingredients:
1 (¼ " thick) ham steak
2 tablespoons margarine
2 tablespoons strong black coffee
4 tablespoons water
Directions:
Melt margarine in a skillet over medium heat.
Add the ham and fry for 6–8 minutes until done. Take off the ham from skillet.
Put coffee and water to the ham juice.
Bring to a boil. Serve the gravy over the ham steak.
Nutrition: 214 calories; 17.1 g total fat; 41 mg cholesterol; 984 mg sodium. 0.6 g carbohydrates; 13.7 g protein; 5

CRACKER BARREL MEAT LOAF

Preparation time: 10 minutes **Cooking time**: 30 minutes Serving: 6
Ingredients
600 g of organic minced meat mixed
1 large onion
2 cloves of garlic
½ green pepper
1 egg
1 handful of crushe d Scandinavian crispy bread
1 tablespoon of potato starch
2 tablespoons of pine nuts
1 handful of basil
sprigs of lemon thyme
large stalks of parsley
2 teaspoons mustard
2 teaspoons paprika powder
1 pinch (s) of salt, pepper
Directions
1 Preheat the oven to 180 ° top/bottom heat.
2 Chop onion, cloves of garlic, and herbs. Cut the dried tomatoes into small pieces. Peel the potato and cut it into small pieces using a kitchen grater (or food processor).
3 Place all ingredients in a large bowl and knead with your hands until everything is well mixed. Season with salt and pepper vigorously.
4 Squeeze the minced meat mass tightly and shape it into a somewhat elongated loaf.
5 Place the meatloaf in a greased baking tin (ideally a tin with a lid) and bake on the middle shelf for approx. 50 minutes until the meatloaf has browned nicely.
Nutrition: Calories: 308 Cal Fat: 2 g Carbs: 70 g Protein: 23 g Fiber: 32 g

QUESADILLA BURGER

Preparation time: 15 minutes Cooking time: 15 minutes Servings: 4
Ingredients:

- 1 1/2pounds ground beef 8 (6-inch) flour tortillas 1 tablespoon butter
- Tex-Mex seasoning for the burgers
- 2 Teaspoons ground cumin 2 Tablespoons paprika 1 Teaspoon black pepper
- ½ Teaspoon cayenne pepper, more or less depending on taste
- 1 Teaspoon salt or to taste 1 tablespoon dried oregano

Toppings

- 8 slices pepper jack cheese 4 slices Applewood-smoked bacon, cooked and crumbled
- 1/2cup shredded iceberg lettuce - Pico de Galo
- 1-2 Roma tomatoes, deseeded and diced thin
- ½-1 tablespoon thinly diced onion (red or yellow is fine) 1-2 Teaspoons fresh lime juice
- 1-2 Teaspoons fresh cilantro, chopped finely
- 1-2 Teaspoons thinly diced jalapeños pepper
- Salt and pepper to taste

Tex-Mex ranch dressing

- 1/2cup sour cream 1/2cup ranch dressing such as Hidden Valley
- 1 Teaspoon Tex-Mex seasoning ¼ Cup mild salsa
- Pepper to taste

For serving (optional)

- Guacamole, and sour cream

Directions:

In a mixing bowl, combine the Tex-Mex seasoning **ingredients** and stir to ensure they are well combined. Prepare the fresh Pico de Gallo by mixing all the **ingredients** in a bowl. Set aside in the refrigerator until ready to use. Prepare the Tex-Mex ranch dressing by mixing all the **ingredients** in a bowl. Set aside in the refrigerator until ready to use. Add 2 Tablespoons of the Tex-Mex seasoning to the ground beef and mix it in, being careful not to overwork the beef or your burgers will be tough. Form into 4 large ¼-inch thick burger patties and cook either on the grill or in a skillet to your preference. Heat a clean skillet over medium-low heat. Butter each of the flour tortillas on one side. Place one butter side down in the skillet. Top with 1 slice of cheese, some shredded lettuce, some Pico de Gallo, some bacon, and then top with a cooked burger. Top the burger with some of the Tex-Mex ranch dressing sauce to taste, some Pico the Gallo, bacon, and another slice of cheese. Cover with another tortilla, butter side up. Cook for about 1 minute or until the tortilla is golden. Then carefully flip the tortilla and cook until the cheese has melted. This step can be done in a sandwich press if you have one. Cut the tortillas in quarters or halves and serve with a side of the Tex-Mex ranch dressing, guacamole, and sour cream, if desired.

Nutrition: Calories: : 1330, Total Fat: 93 g, Cholesterol: 240 mg, Sodium: : 3000 mg, Total Carbohydrate: 50 g, Dietary Fiber: 6 g, Sugar: s: 7 g, Protein: : 74g

CHAPTER 6

DESSERT AND BEVERAGE

CHOCOLATE CHERRY COBBLER
Preparation Time: 10 minutes
Cooking Time: 45 minutes
Servings: 8
Ingredients:
1. 1 can (21 oz.) cherry pie filling
2. 1½ cups flour½ cup sugar
3. 2 tsp baking powder
4. ½ tsp salt¼ Cup
5. (½ stick) cold butter
6. 1 Egg
7. 1 cup (a 6 oz. bag) chocolate chips
8. ¼ Cup evaporated milk
9. ½ cup slivered almonds

Directions:
1. Preheat oven to 350 degrees F. You will need a 1½ to 2-quart baking dish (I used a 1.5 QT oval).
2. Mix flour, sugar, salt & baking powder in a medium bowl. Cut butter into chunks and add to the flour mixture.
3. Cut in butter until the mixture resembles small peas. Set aside. Spread cherry pie filling in the bottom of a 1.5 to 2-quart baking dish. Set aside. Melt chocolate chips either in the microwave or stovetop. Stir frequently until the chips are all melted, and mixture is smooth. Cool for about 5 minutes. Add evaporated milk and egg to melted chocolate chips. Stir until well blended. Add the chocolate mixture to the flour mixture. Mix very well. Drop randomly on top of cherry filling in baking dish. Sprinkle with the almonds. Bake at 350 degrees F for 40-45 minutes. Serve warm with ice cream, whipped cream, or cream.

Nutrition:
Calories: : 460 Carbs: 15g Fat: 19g Protein: : 6g Fiber: 3g

APPLE DUMPLING BAKE
Preparation Time: 15 minutes
Cooking Time: 35 minutes
Servings: 8
Ingredients:

- 2 medium Granny Smith apples
- 2 tubes (8 ounces each) refrigerated crescent rolls
- 1 cup sugar
- 1/3 cup butter,
- Softened ½ teaspoon ground cinnamon
- 3/4 Cup Mountain Dew soda
- Vanilla ice cream

Directions:
1. Preheat oven to 350°. Peel, core and cut each apple into 8 wedges. Unroll both tubes of crescent dough; separate each into 8 triangles. Wrap a triangle around each wedge. Place in a greased 13x9-in. baking dish.
2. In a bowl, mix sugar, butter, and cinnamon until blended, sprinkle over dumplings. Slowly pour soda around the rolls (do not stir).
3. Bake, uncovered, until golden brown and apples are tender, 35-40 minutes. Serve warm with ice cream.

Nutrition:
Calories: : 414 Carbs: 10g Fat: 20g Protein: : 4g Fiber: 1g

HOMEMADE CORN MUFFINS WITH HONEY BUTTER

Preparation Time: 20 minutes
Cooking Time: 20 minutes
Servings: 1
Ingredients:

- 1/4 cup butter, softened
- 1/4 cup reduced-fat cream cheese 1
- /2 cup sugar
- 2 large eggs
- 1-½ cups fat-free milk
- 1-½ cups all-purpose flour
- 1-½ cups yellow cornmeal
- 4 teaspoons baking powder
- ¾ teaspoon salt

Honey Butter:

- 2 Tablespoons honey

Directions:

1. In a large bowl, cream the butter, cream cheese, and sugar until light and fluffy.
2. Add eggs, one at a time, beating well after each addition.
3. Stir in the milk. Combine the flour, cornmeal, baking powder and salt; add to creamed mixture just until moistened. Coat muffin cups with cooking spray; fill three-fourths full of batter. Bake at 400° for 18-22 minutes or until a toothpick inserted in the center comes out clean. Cool for 5 Minutes before removing from pans to wire racks.
4. Beat butter and honey until blended; serve with warm muffins.

Nutrition:
Calories: : 198 Carbs: 19g Fat: 7g Protein: : 4g

PEACH COBBLER WITH ALMOND CRUMBLE TOPPING

Preparation Time: 15 minutes
Cooking Time: 1 hour
Servings: 6-9
Ingredients:
Batter

- 1 cup cracker barrel pancake mix
- 1 cup milk
- ½ cup melted butter
- ¼ teaspoon nutmeg
- ½ Teaspoon cinnamon

Filling

- 2 (15 ounce) cans peach slices in heavy syrup or (15 ounce) cans diced peaches in heavy syrup
- ¼ Cup sugar
- Topping
- ½ cup brown sugar
- 1/8 cup flour
- ½ Teaspoon cinnamon
- 1 tablespoon softened butter
- Sliced almonds

Directions:

1. Mix all batter ingredients in a bowl with whisk until well incorporated and light. Pour into non greased 8 x 8 baking pan.
2. Drain peaches of syrup except for about a tablespoon of juice in each can and mix with sugar until it has dissolved. Pour over batter but do not mix -- batter will rise over peaches and juices on its own.
3. Mix all topping ingredients with hands slightly breaking up almonds as you incorporate. Do not place on cobbler yet as the almonds will burn! That step will come well along.
4. Place into 375-degree oven for 45 minutes. Then, while leaving cobbler in oven, place crumble topping over cobbler and bake another 10-15 minutes. Watch carefully so that nuts do not burn.
5. Serve while still a little warm with some cinnamon ice cream and enjoy!

Nutrition:
Calories: : 475.1 Carbs: 17.2g Fat: 20.1g Protein: : 4.8g

BANANA PUDDING
Preparation Time: 10 Minutes
Cooking Time: 30 minutes
Servings: 6
Ingredients:
Pudding

- 3/4 Cup sugar
- 1/3 cup all-purpose flour
- 3 Cups whole milk
- 4 beaten egg yolks
- 3 tablespoons butter
- 2 ounces cream cheese
- 2 Teaspoons vanilla

Banana Pudding

- 48 vanilla wafers
- 1 cup heavy whipping cream whipped
- 1 Teaspoon sugar
- 2 large bananas

Directions:
Pudding

1. In a heavy saucepan combine sugar, flour, and milk. Cook and stir continually over medium heat until the mixture is thickened and bubbly. Cook and stir for an additional two minutes. Remove from heat.
2. Place for egg yolks in a small bowl. Beat eggs well. Place 1 cup of the hot pudding mixture slowly into the beaten eggs. Stir the egg mixture well, and then slowly add this into the pan where the remainder of the pudding is. Cook the mixture until it just begins to bubble. Add butter, cream cheese, and vanilla. Stir until all of the ingredients are well incorporated.
3. Pour the pudding into a bowl. Place plastic wrap on the surface of the pudding. Place pudding into the refrigerator to cool.

Whipped Cream

4. Place 1 cup of heavy whipping cream into a bowl with 1 Teaspoon of sugar.
5. Using either a whisk or a mixer, beat the whipping cream until it becomes stiff. Refrigerate, and use immediately.
6. Assembling the pudding
7. Break for vanilla wafers into each jar, cut bananas into slices, and place 4 or 5 slices of bananas into each jar.
8. Add a couple of tablespoons of pudding on top of the bananas. Repeat 2 more times in each jar. Top with whipped cream.

Nutrition: Calories: : 723 Carbs: 14g Fat: 39g Protein: : 10g Fiber: 2g

STRAWBERRY SHORTCAKE
Preparation Time: 10 minutes
Cooking Time: 10 minutes
Servings: 8
Ingredients:
- 1 pre-made pound cake
- 1-pint frozen sweetened strawberries
- 4 scoops premium vanilla ice cream
- 1 can whipped cream
- Scratch Method
- 4 scoops vanilla ice cream
- 1 homemade pound cake
- 1-pound Fresh strawberries
- 1-pint whipped cream

Directions:
1. Assemble strawberry shortcake by cutting two slices of the pound cake and then slicing those in half.
2. In a bowl, place the 4 pieces of pound cake across from each other.
3. Spoon defrosted strawberries onto cake; add one scoop of vanilla ice cream and top with whipped cream.
4. While the Cracker Barrel may use frozen strawberries, I really like fresh much more. I think you can jazz up this recipe by using fresh strawberries, fresh whipped cream, and if you are up for it, a homemade pound cake.
5. From Scratch Method
6. Prepare the strawberries several hours ahead of time by cleaning them, slicing them, and placing them into a bowl.
7. Add about 1 tablespoon of superfine sugar, if available, to the strawberries and mix well. Place strawberries in the refrigerator. The sugar will help to make the strawberries juicy.
8. Whip the whipping cream with a mixer until firm. You may want to add a touch of vanilla to this for some extra flavor.
9. When you are ready to serve the shortcakes, follow the Directions: above.

Nutrition:
Calories: : 542 Carbs: 17g Fat: 22g Protein: : 9g Fiber: 3g

APPLE CHIMI CHEESECAKE

Preparation Time: 10 Minutes
Cooking time: 10 Minutes
Servings: 2
Ingredients:

- 2 (9 inch) flour tortillas
- ¼ Cup granulated sugar
- ½ Teaspoon cinnamon
- 3 ounces' cream cheese, softened
- ½ Teaspoon vanilla extract
- 1/3 cup apple, peeled and finely chopped
- Oil for frying
- Vanilla ice cream (optional)
- Caramel topping (optional)

Directions:

1. Make sure your tortillas and cream cheese are at room temperature; this will make them both easier to work with.
2. In a small bowl, combine the sugar and cinnamon.
3. In another mixing bowl, combine the cream cheese and vanilla until smooth. Fold in the apple.
4. Divide the apple and cheese mixture in two and place half in the center of each tortilla. Leave at least an inch margin around the outside.
5. Fold the tortilla top to the middle, then the bottom to the middle, and then roll it up from the sides.
6. Heat about half an inch of oil in a skillet over medium heat.
7. Place the filled tortillas into the skillet and fry on each side until they are golden brown. Transfer them to a paper towel lined plate to drain any excess oil, then immediately coat them with the cinnamon and sugar.
8. Serve with a scoop of ice cream.

Nutrition:
Calories: : 267
Fat: 5g
Carbs: 15g
Protein: : 18g
Sodium: : 276mg

CRACKER BARREL'S BAKED APPLE DUMPLIN COPYCAT

Preparation Time: 10 minutes
Cooking Time: 20 minutes
Servings: 4
Ingredients
2 medium Granny Smith apples
2 tubes (8 ounces each) refrigerated crescent rolls
1 cup sugar
1/3 cup butter, softened
1/2 teaspoon ground cinnamon
3/4 cup Mountain Dew soda
Vanilla ice cream
Directions:
Oven preheat to 350 ° C. Each apple is peel, core, and cut into 8 wedges. Unroll all Crescent dough tubes; divide each into eight triangles. Wrap each wedge around a triangle. Place yourself in a greased 13x9in. Baking platter.
Mix the sugar, butter and cinnamon in a bowl until mixed; scatter over dumplings. Slowly pour in soda (do not stir) around the rolls.
Bake uncovered, for 3540 minutes, until golden brown and apples are tender. With the ice cream, serve warm.
Nutrition: calories 383, fat 14, fiber 4, carbs 3, protein 8

CRACKER BARREL FRIED APPLES WITH NUTMEG

Preparation time: 10 minutes
Cooking time: 25 minutes
Serving: 8
Ingredients:
8 red apples
¼ pound butter
½ cup of sugar
1 teaspoon cinnamon
Dash of nutmeg
Directions:
Do not peel the apples. Slice the apples into slices about ½" thick. Melt the butter in a skillet in medium heat. Add the apples and sugar to the skillet. Place a lid on the skillet and cook for 20 minutes, or until the apples are tender and juicy. Sprinkle with cinnamon and nutmeg before serving.
Nutrition: Calories 172.6 Sodium 6.1 mg Carbohydrate 44.3 g Protein 0.5 g

SPICED BAKED APPLES LIKE CRACKER BARREL'S

Preparation Time: 20 Minutes
Cooking Time: 15 Minutes
Servings: 6
Ingredients:
2 cups apple juice, plus
1/2 cup apple juice
4 large Golden Delic ious apples
3 tablespoons cornstarch
1 teaspoon apple pie spice
4 tablespoons sugar
Directions:
Core and cut apples into 1/2 inch wedges.
In a medium skillet, combine the 2 cups apple juice and sliced apples.
Simmer gently until apples are fork tender but not mushy, turning apples frequently.
Remove apples from juice using a slotted spoon and place in an oven safe dish.
In a blender, combine the remaining 1/2 cup apple juice, cornstarch, apple pie spice and sugar.
Blend a few seconds until smooth.
Whisk mixture into hot apple juice in skillet and cook for approximately 15 minutes, stirring constantly on medium high heat until it bubbles and becomes thickened and smooth.
Pour thickened mixture over apples and serve.
Nutrition:
Calories: 175 kcal
Protein: 0.54 g
Fat: 0.38 g
Carbohydrates: 42.48 g

CRACKER BARREL CHOCOLATE PECAN PIE

Preparation Time: 20 Minutes
Cooking Time: 15 Minutes
Servings: 6
Ingredients
1 plain pastry shell
1 cup pecans
3 tablespoons semisweet chocolate chips
3 eggs, beaten
½ cup sugar
1 cup corn syrup
½ teaspoon salt
1 teaspoon vanilla extract
¼ cup melted margarine
Directions
Preheat oven to 350°F.
Arrange pecan nuts in pie shell and sprinkle with chocolate chips.
Add sugar to eggs and beat well.
Add the remaining ingredients and mix until wellblended.
Pour mixture over pecans.
Bake until knife inserted in center comes out clean (about 50–60 minutes, or with an internal temperature of 200°F).
Cool completely to set.
Nutrition: Calories 345, Total Fat 38 g, Carbs 58 g, Protein 6 g, Sodium 350 mg

CRACKER BARREL™ COPYCAT CHOCOLATE CHERRY COBBLER

Preparation Time: 20 Minutes
Cooking Time: 35 Minutes
Servings: 6
Ingredients:
Cherry pie filling (21 oz. can)
Allpurpose flour (1.5 cups)
Baking powder (2 tsp.)
Salt (.5 tsp.)
Sugar (.5 cup)
Cold butter (.25 cup or half of 1 stick)
Egg (1)
Evaporated milk (.25 cup)
Chocolate chips (6 oz. bag or 1 cup)
Slivered almonds (.5 cup)
Also Recommended: 1.52quart oval baking dish
Directions:
Warm the oven to reach 350° Fahrenheit.
Sift the flour, salt, baking powder, and sugar in a mixing container. Cutin the butter chunks until it's peasized. Set aside for now.
Dump the filling into the baking dish. Set it aside also.
Melt the chocolate chips and stir until melted using the microwave or stovetop. Cool it down for about five minutes. Mix in the milk and egg. Stir.
Combine the flour and chocolate fixings and drop into the cherry filling in the baking dish.
Sprinkle using the almonds and set the timer for 4045 minutes.
Serve warm with whipped cream or ice cream.
Nutrition: calories 260, fat 25, fiber 2, carbs 8, protein 2

CRACKER BARREL'S DOUBLE FUDGE COCA COLA CHOCOLATE CAKE

Preparation Time: 20 Minutes **Cooking Time**: 15 Minutes **Servings**: 6

Ingredients

1 cup coca cola
1/2 cup vegetable oil
1/2 cup (1 stick) salted butter
3 heapingish tablespoons dark cocoa powder
2 cups granulated sugar
2 cups allpurpose flour
2 large eggs
1/2 cup buttermilk
1 teaspoon baking soda
1 teaspoon vanilla extract
1 stick salted butter
3 tablespoons dark cocoa powder
6 tablespoons milk
1 teaspoon vanilla extract
4 cups powdered sugar

Directions:

Preheat oven to 350°F.

Butter and flour a 9x13 pan and set aside. In the big bowl of a mixer, stir together sugar and flour and set aside. In a saucepan, convey cola, oil, butter, and cocoa to a boil. Pour into the flour combination and beat on mediumlow for approximately till a toothpick inserted in the middle comes out clean. Immediately upon eliminating cake from the oven, put together with frosting.

In a saucepan over medium heat, deliver butter, cocoa powder, and milk to simply boiling. Remove from warmth and whisk in powdered sugar and vanilla. Pour over cake and quick unfold. Let cake cool to room temperature, then cowl and refrigerate until serving.

Nutrition

Carbohydrates: 46g Protein: 2g Fat: 16g

CRACKER BARREL BANANA PUDDING

Preparation Time10 minutes
Cooking time 50 minutes
Servings 4
INGREDIENTS
1½ quarts milk
11/8 cups flour
1¼ cups liquid egg substitute
¼ cup vanilla extract
12 ounces vanilla wafers
1 (8ounce) container
1¼ cups sugar
1¾ peeled bananas
Cool Whip
1. Warm up the milk in a 170 ° F saucepan.
2. Blend the eggs, flour, vanilla, and sugar in a cup.
3. In the saucepan add the sugar mixture to the milk.
4. Cook, stirring continuously, for 10–12 minutes until it is custard like.
5. Spread the wafers down the baking pan.
6. Cut the bananas and put on the wafers.
7. Pour the custard over the bananas and the wafers.
8. Let it cool, then add Cool Whip to the top.
Nutrition: calories 160, fat 5.4, fiber 2, carbs 4.3, protein 3.9

CRACKER BARREL CARROT CAKE

Preparation Time10 minutes **Cooking time** 50 minutes **Servings** 4
Ingredients
3 cups flour
2 teaspoons baking soda
2 teaspoons baking powder - ½ teaspoon salt
1 teaspoon ground nutmeg - 2 teaspoons ground cinnamon
½ teaspoon ground cloves
1½ cups sugar - 1¼ cups vegetable oil
½ cup brown sugar - 3 eggs
2 teaspoons vanilla
1 cup crushed pineapple
½ cup shredded coconut
¾ cup finely chopped walnuts
2 cups shredded carrots
½ cup chopped pecans, for garnish
Cream Cheese Frosting
½ cup raisins - 8 ounces cream cheese
1 teaspoon vanilla - ½ cup roomtemperature butter
2 cups powdered sugar
Directions
1. Preheat the oven to 350 ° F.
2. Mix the flour, baking powder, baking soda, salt, cinnamon, nutmeg, cloves together. Put aside.
3. Mix the oil, sugars, vanilla, and eggs in a large bowl, using a beater, until smooth and fluffy. Stir in the pineapple, walnuts, coconut, carrots, and raisins and combine well. Gradually add half of the flour mixture at a time, until combined. Pour the batter into a thick and floured pan of 9" by 13" and bake for about 40–50 minutes. Check for doneness using toothpick. Mix the cream cheese and butter, until light and fluffy, to create the frosting. Apply the vanilla and a little powdered sugar at one time until everything has mixed well. Turn the mixer up and beat until light and fluffy to frost.Spread the icing over the refrigerated cake and sprinkle with pecans
Nutrition: calories 260, fat 4.4, fiber 3, carbs 7, protein 10

CRACKER BARREL™ STYLE FRIED APPLES IN A SKILLET

Preparation Time 10 minutes
Cooking time 40 minutes
Servings 4
Ingredients:
Butter (3 tbsp.)
Golden Delicious apples (4 medium)
Granulated sugar (.25 cup)
Cinnamon (1 tsp.)
Nutmeg (.25 tsp.)
Packed brown sugar (2 tbsp.)
Apple cider (.5 cup)
Cornstarch (1 tbsp.)
Also Needed: 12inch skillet
Directions:
Core and slice the apples into about two pounds of ¾inch wedges.
Melt the butter in a skillet using the medium heat setting.
Toss in the apples, spices, and sugar. Stir and place a lid on the pan.
Simmer for 1114 minutes, occasionally stirring until tenderized.
Scoop into a serving dish to keep warm.
Whisk the cider and cornstarch together and pour into the skillet.
Simmer using medium heat for 3060 seconds until it's thickened.
Pour the mixture over the apples before serving.
Nutrition: calories 300, fat 8.3, fiber 3.3, carbs 6, protein 13

KETO DIET/OPTION WITH LOW CARB

CHAPTER 7

BREAKFAST KETO OPTION

BURRITO
Preparation Time: 15 minutes
Cooking Time: 20 minutes
Servings: 10
Ingredients:
- 1 pound pork sausage mild
- 1/2 cup yellow onion diced
- 1/4 cup fresh tomatoes diced
- One tablespoon of green chilies
- 10 — tortillas
- Nine eggs
- 6 ounces American cheese 12 sliced pieces
- 1/2 cup salsa

Directions:
1. Crumble and fry the pork sausage, stir and break the meat in small parts to cook.
2. Place drained sausage in the frying pan. Add the onion, green chilies and tomatoes, heat up at medium temperature until sausage and vegetables are cooked through. Stir from time to time.
3. Measure and beat 2 cups of eggs. Add the eggs and the sausage mixture to the pan. When finished, take off from the heat.
4. Then place sausages and egg mixture (2 tablespoons) on one tortilla. Break each slice of American cheese into two even portions, then put the cheese onto the sausage mixture, and roll the tortilla.
5. If you do all of these ahead of time, you can wrap them in plastic to put them in the refrigerator or freezer, and then heat them for a moment or two in the microwave.
6. Serve with the taco or picante sauce, as you like. You will find these are milder for breakfast and very significant.

Nutrition
Calories: 269 kcal, Carbohydrates: 3 g,
Protein: 15 g, Fat: 21 g,
Saturated Fat: 8 g, Cholesterol: 196

EGG MCMUFFIN SANDWICH

Preparation Time 10 minutes   Cooking Time 20 minutes   Serving: 5

Ingredients:

- 6 English muffins
- Eight spoonfuls of salted butter
- 12 slices American cheese
- 12 large eggs
- Six slices Canadian bacon

Directions:

1. The oven should be preheated to the temperature of 300 ° F.
2. Fry the eggs until they are fried well, using a round egg mold if you just want a round egg. Warm the Canadian sliced bacon by frying it on the griddle, too.
3. Slice in half the English muffins, then toast them in a toaster.
4. Place a thin layer of butter on each half of the English toasted muffin.
5. In every English muffin, add a slice of cheese to the bottom half.
6. Place the English muffins on a sheet of cookies and into the oven, allowing the cheese to melt slightly; it will take only about 3 to 5 minutes.
7. Remove from the oven the English muffins, and start layering. You must add an egg to the coated bottom of the sandwich, add another layer of cheese onto the egg, add a second egg, then a slice of Canadian bacon, followed by the top of the English muffin.
8. Serve warm, and enjoy!

Nutrition:

Calories: 558, Total Fat: 36g,
Saturated Fat: 18g, Trans Fat: 1g,
Unsaturated Fat: 14g, Cholesterol: 453mg,
Carbohydrates: 3 g,

TACO BELL CRUNCH WRAP

Preparation: 20 minutes
Cooking Time: 10 minutes
Servings: 2
Ingredients:

- Two flour tortillas
- Three eggs
- Two spoonfuls shredded Cheddar cheese
- 1/2 cup hash browns -2 fried hash brown patties
- Four spoonfuls Taco Bell Sauce
- Four bacon pieces, cooked and crunchy

Directions:

1. Prepare scrambled eggs by splitting into a bowl three full eggs and whisking them with a fork. Pour eggs over medium heat into a non-stick skillet that you coated with non-stick spray.
2. Season the eggs with salt and pepper, and mix the eggs in the saucepan until thoroughly cooked. Remove eggs from the burner and set aside. Use a large skillet for cooking the tortillas over medium heat. Lay a tortilla in the skillet, and warm-up for about 30 seconds on each side.
3. You want the tortilla to be quite pliable. Start by adding 1/4 cup cooked hash browns or one cooked hash brown patty to create the crunch package. Add half the eggs, two tablespoons of taco bell sauce, one tablespoon milk, and two crumbled bits of bacon.
4. Turn the side nearest to you, to the middle to close Crunch Wrap, then turn right and left to the bottom—end by closing the top of the crunch wrap by closing the center to the right and left. You'll finish off with a five-sided tie. Add some non-stick spray to the skillet you used to cook the tortilla in, then heat up on medium heat for around 30-40 seconds. Turn the wrap and heat on the other side. They will look golden brown on both sides.

Nutrition:
Calories: 480kcal, Carbohydrates: 8g,
Protein: 21g, Fat: 31g,
Saturated Fat: 11g, Cholesterol: 290mg,
Sodium: 919mg,

SPINACH AND CHEESE EGG SOUFFLÉ

Preparation Time: 15 minutes Cooking Time: 25 minutes Servings: 4

Ingredients:

1 tube butter flake crescent rolls

6 eggs, divided

3 tablespoons milk

2 tablespoons heavy cream

¼ cup cheddar cheese, grated

¼ cup jack cheese, grated

1 tablespoon Parmesan cheese

3 tablespoons fresh spinach, mince

4 slices of bacon, cooked and crumbled

Cooking spray

¼ teaspoon salt

¼ cup Asiago cheese, grated, divided

Directions:

Preheat oven to 375°F.

Add 5 eggs, milk, heavy cream, cheddar cheese, jack cheese, parmesan cheese, spinach, bacon, and salt to a nonreactive bowl. Mix well until combined then heat in microwave for about 30 seconds. Stir, then microwave for another 20 seconds. Repeat about 5 times or until egg mixture is a bit thicker but still runny and uncooked.

Roll out crescent roll dough. Make 4 rectangles by pressing together the triangles. Then, using a roll pin, stretch them out until they are 6in x 6in square.

Coat ramekin with cooking spray and place flattened roll inside, making sure the edges are outside the ramekin. Add ⅓ cup egg mixture and then about ⅛ cup Asiago cheese. Wrap edges of the roll-on top. Repeat for remaining rolls.

Whisk remaining egg with salt lightly in a bowl then, with a pastry brush, brush on top of each crescent roll dough. Place ramekins in the oven and bake for 20 minutes or until brown. Serve.

Nutrition:

Calories: 303 Fat: 25 g Saturated Fat: 11 g Carbs: 4 g Sugar: 1 g Fibers: 0 g Protein: 20 g Sodium: 749 mg

GLAZED DONUTS

Preparation Time: 30 minutes **Cooking Time:** 2 hours **Servings:** 7
Ingredients:
For the Donut Batter,

- Five cups of flour (all-purpose)
- Four and a half tsps. of instant yeast
- One and a half cup of low fat or whole milk
- One tsp. of salt
- Two eggs (large in size)
- One-third cup of warm water (40-46C or 105-115F)
- Half cup of granulated sugar
- One-third cup of soft butter/shortening (nearly 75g)
- Canola oil (needed for frying)

For the Donut glaze,

- Five-seven tbsps. of evaporated milk
- Half cup of melted butter
- Two tsps. of vanilla
- Two cups of sugar (powdered)

Directions:

1. Take a standing mixer and mix yeast and lukewarm water. Keep it undisturbed for nearly five minutes until it dissolves.
2. In the meantime, heat milk in a medium-sized microwave-safe bowl for two minutes. Allow it to cool. Now, add eggs, milk, salt, sugar, two cups flour, butter, or shortening to the yeast bowl. Mix all the **ingredients** properly at a medium speed. Then, pour three cups flour and keep mixing the dough.
3. As it is done, take a large-sized greased bowl and place the dough in it. Cover the bowl loosely with a cloth and keep it in a warm place for nearly one-two hours. By doing so, the dough will rise. Sprinkle flour on a clean surface and then roll the dough to a thickness of about a quarter inch. Start cutting the donuts with a cookie cutter or donut cutter of about one inch. Allow it to stand for ten minutes. Meanwhile, pour canola oil (minimum three inches high) into a large-sized saucepan and place it on medium heat. Heat the oil until it is 375 degrees.
4. Drop a few donuts into the hot oil very carefully. Turn the donuts once and fry for three minutes till they are golden brown in color. Keep the fried donuts on paper towels.
5. As soon as you are done with frying, melt butter in a bowl (microwave safe).
6. Remove the bowl and add vanilla extract and powdered sugar into it. Keep stirring until all the **ingredients** mix evenly. Next, you need to add evaporated milk until you get a perfect consistency. Now, dip all the donuts in the glaze. Allow them to drip on a rack. Mouthwatering glazed donuts are ready to be served.

Nutrition: Calories: 228 | Carbs: 35g| Fat: 8g| Protein: 3g | Fiber: 1g

BISCUITS AND SAUSAGE GRAVY

Preparation Time: 5 minutes
Cooking Time: 10 minutes
Servings: 2
Ingredients:

- 2-3 tbsps. of flour (all-purpose flour can be used)
- Warm biscuits
- A quarter-pound of bulk pork sausage
- One and a quarter cups of whole milk
- Two tbsps. of butter
- One-eighth tsp. of pepper
- A quarter tsp. of salt

Directions:

1. Firstly, take a clean and small skillet for cooking the sausage on medium heat. Cook till the pink color of the sausage is gone.
2. Quickly add the butter and start heating until it melts.
3. Now, add flour, pepper, and salt. Keep stirring until it blends nicely.
4. Slowly add milk and stir continuously. Let it boil, stir, and cook for nearly two minutes till it thickens. Serve with warm biscuits.

Note: For enhancing the flavor of your gravy, you may add fresh herbs such as parsley. If you want, then you can substitute whole milk with skim milk or heavy cream.

Nutrition:

Calories: 337 | Carbs: 8g | Fat: 27 | Protein: 10g | Fiber: 1g

EGGS BENEDICT FROM MIMI CAFÉ

Preparation Time: 10 minutes
Cooking Time: 20 minutes
Servings: 8
Ingredients:

- Three-fourth cup of melted butter
- White pepper
- Two tbsps. lemon juice
- Two tbsps. water
- Four egg yolks

For the assembly,

- Eight slices of warmed Canadian bacon
- Four split and toasted English muffins
- Eight eggs
- Paprika

Directions:

1. For making the hollandaise sauce, take a metal bowl over the simmering water, or you can also take a double boiler. Then add the egg yolks, lemon juice, and water and whisk them until they are smoothly blended. Allow it to cook until the temperature reaches 160 degrees, and the mixture becomes thick enough for coating a metal spoon accompanied by constant whisking. Then whisk in some pepper. Then, if necessary, transfer it to a small bowl. Then place this bowl inside a large bowl containing hot water. Keeping it warm, stir occasionally for about thirty minutes until it becomes ready to serve
2. Take a large skillet or saucepan having high sides. Then pour water up to two to three inches. Then bring it to a boil and then adjust the heat for maintaining a gentle simmer. Then take a small bowl and break an egg. Then gently slip the egg to the water. Do the same thing for three more eggs.
3. Cook it for about three to four minutes while keeping it uncovered, until the egg yolks become thick (not hard though), and the egg whites are completely set. Then use a slotted spoon and lift the eggs out of the water. Do this for all the four eggs.
4. Top all the muffin halves with a poached egg, a slice of bacon, and two tbsps. of sauce. Sprinkle each muffin half with paprika. Then serve.

Nutrition:
Calories: 345 | Carbs: 15g | Fat: 26g | Protein: 13g | Fiber: 1g

TASTY EGGS AND SAUSAGES

Preparation Time: 10 minutes
Cooking Time: 35 minutes
Servings: 6
Ingredients:

- 12 eggs
- 5 tablespoons ghee
- 1-ounce spinach, torn
- Salt and black pepper to the taste
- 12 ham slices
- 1 yellow onion, chopped
- 2 sausages, chopped
- 1 red bell pepper, chopped

Directions:

1. Firstly, heat up a pan with 1 tablespoon ghee over medium heat, add sausages and onion, stir and cook for 5 minutes.
2. Add bell pepper, salt and pepper, stir and cook for 3 minutes more and transfer to a bowl.
3. Melt the rest of the ghee and divide into 12 cupcake molds.
4. Add a slice of ham in each cupcake mold, divide spinach in each and then the sausage mix
5. Crack an egg on top, introduce everything in the oven and bake at 425 degrees F for 20 minutes.
6. Leave your keto cupcakes to cool down a bit before serving.
7. Enjoy!

Nutrition:
Calories: 440 | Carbs: 12g Protein: 22g | Fiber: 0g

KETO BREAKFAST FRENCH TOAST

Preparation Time: 5 minutes
Cooking Time: 45 minutes
Servings: 18
Ingredients:

- 12 egg whites
- 1 cup whey protein
- 4 ounces cream cheese

For the French toast:

- ½ cup coconut milk
- 1 teaspoon vanilla
- 2 eggs
- ½ cup ghee, melted
- 1 teaspoon cinnamon, ground
- ½ cup almond milk
- ½ cup swerve

Directions:

1. Mix 12 egg whites with your mixer for a few minutes in a bowl.
2. Then add protein and stir gently.
3. Add cream cheese and stir.
4. Put this into 2 greased bread pans, cook it in the oven at 325 degrees F and bake for 45 minutes.
5. Leave bread to cool down and slice them into pieces.
6. In a bowl, mix 2 eggs with vanilla, cinnamon, coconut milk and whisk well.
7. Dip bread slices in this mix.
8. Heat up a pan with some coconut oil over medium heat, then add bread slices. Cook until they are golden on each side and transfer them in plates
9. Heat up a pan with the ghee over high heat, add almond milk.
10. Add swerve, stir and take off heat.
11. Then cool it down a bit and drizzle over French toasts.
12. Enjoy!

Nutrition:
Calories: 200 | Carbs: 1g | Fat: 6g | Protein: 7g | Fiber: 1g

DELICIOUS LOW CARB PANCAKES
Preparation Time: 3 minutes
Cooking Time: 12 minutes
Servings: 4
Ingredients:
- 1 teaspoon stevia
- ½ teaspoon cinnamon, ground
- Cooking spray
- 2 eggs
- 2 ounces cream cheese

Directions:
1. Blend eggs with cream cheese, stevia and cinnamon in your blender.
2. Heat up a pan with some cooking spray over medium high heat, put ¼ of the batter, spread well, cook for 2 minutes, flip and cook for 1 minute more.
3. Place on a plate and repeat the action with the rest of the batter.
4. Serve them.
5. Enjoy!

Nutrition:
Calories: 344 | Carbs: 3g | Fat: 23g | Protein: 16g | Fiber: 12g

LOW CARB ALMOND PANCAKES

Preparation Time: 10 minutes
Cooking Time: 10 minutes;
Servings: 12
Ingredients:

- A pinch of salt
- 6 eggs
- ½ cup coconut flour
- 1/3 cup coconut, shredded
- ¼ cup stevia
- ½ teaspoon baking powder
- ¼ cup coconut oil
- 1 cup almond milk
- 1 teaspoon almond extract
- 2 ounces cocoa chocolate
- ¼ cup almonds, toasted
- Cooking spray

Directions:

1. Mix coconut flour with stevia, baking powder, salt, coconut and stir.
2. Then add coconut oil, almond milk eggs and the almond extract and stir well.
3. Add almonds and chocolate and then whisk well again.
4. Heat up a pan with cooking spray over medium heat, add 2 tablespoons batter, spread into a circle, cook until it's golden, flip, cook again until it's done and transfer to a pan.
5. Repeat with the rest of the batter and serve your pancakes right away.
6. Enjoy!

Nutrition:
Calories: 266 | Carbs: 10g | Fat: 13g | Fiber: 8g

CHAPTER 8

LUNCH AND DINNER KETO OPTION

APPLE PECAN SALAD WITH CHICKEN

Preparation Time: 10 minutes **Cooking Time:** 10 minutes **Servings:** ½ salad

Ingredients:

- 2 tablespoons vegetable oil
- 2 chicken breasts
- 2 cups Romaine lettuce
- 1 cup spinach
- ¼ cup strawberries (sliced)
- ¼ cup cranberries (dried)
- 2 tablespoons pecans (chopped)
- ½ cup bleu cheese crumbles
- ¼ teaspoon parsley (dried)
- ¼ teaspoon garlic powder
- ¼ teaspoon Himalayan sea salt
- ¼ teaspoon black pepper

Directions:

1. Place a medium-sized skillet onto the stove and turn the heat to medium high. Add the oil to the skillet and allow it to get hot.
2. As the skillet is heating up, take a small mixing bowl and add the garlic powder, parsley, sea salt, and black pepper. Stir until well combined.
3. Take each of the chicken breasts and sprinkle on the garlic powder mixture on all sides.
4. Place your seasoned chicken breast into the skillet. Cook the chicken for five minutes then flip and cook for another five minutes. Once the internal temperature of the chicken has reached 165 degrees Fahrenheit, remove from the skillet and allow it to rest on a cutting board.
5. While the chicken is resting, prepare the rest of your salad. In a large salad bowl add the spinach, lettuce, strawberries, and cranberries. Toss everything together with salad spoons. Divide the salad into two equal portions and top each portion with half the pecans and bleu cheese. Slice the chicken breast and place on top of your salad. Serve with your preferred keto-friendly salad dressing.

Nutrition: Calories: 538 | Carbs: 5g | Fat: 46g | Protein: 24g

IN-N-OUT BURGER

Preparation Time: 10 minutes
Cooking Time: 10 minutes **Servings:** 1 burger **Ingredients:**

- 1 ½ pounds lean ground beef
- 5 slices cheddar cheese
- 20 lettuce leaves
- 1 teaspoon Himalayan sea salt
- 1 teaspoon black pepper
- *optional toppings:
- tomato slices
- onion slices
- pickle slices
- For the Sauce:
- ½ cup mayonnaise
- 1 tablespoon sugar-free ketchup
- 1 teaspoon mustard paste
- 2 tablespoons pickles (diced)
- 2 teaspoon pickle juice
- ½ teaspoon paprika
- ½ teaspoon garlic powder
- ½ teaspoon Himalayan sea salt

Directions:

1. Begin by preparing the sauce. Combine the mayonnaise, sugar-free ketchup, mustard paste, diced pickles and pickle juice, paprika, garlic powder, and sea salt into a medium mixing bowl. Whisk everything together thoroughly, cover the bowl with plastic wrap, and store in the refrigerator until ready.
2. Next, you want to place a griddle pan or grill pan on your stove. Add a little bit of oil or cooking spray to the pan and turn the heat to medium, so it gets nice and hot as you prepare your patties.
3. In a large mixing bowl, add your ground beef, sea salt, and black pepper. Use your hands to mix everything together. Portion out the meat into five equal servings and roll them into a ball form then flatten slightly to form your patties. Place your patties onto your hot griddle and cook for 5 minutes on each side or until they turn a dark brown color.
4. When the burgers are done cooking, turn the heat off the stove and top the patties with your cheddar cheese slices.
5. To assemble your patties, lay two leaves of lettuce down first. Place your burger patty on the lettuce leaf, top with your favorite burger toppings, then take the sauce you prepared early and drizzle it over top. Place another two lettuce leaves on top and enjoy!

Nutrition:
Calories: 466 | Carbs: 5g| Fat: 26g | Protein: 48.5g

BUFFALO WILD WINGS SPICY GARLIC SAUCE CHICKEN WINGS

Preparation Time: 10 minutes
Cooking Time: 50 minutes
Servings: ¼ recipe
Ingredients:

- 2 ½ pounds chicken wings
- ½ teaspoon Himalayan sea salt
- For Sauce:
- ¼ cup avocado oil
- ½ cup hot sauce
- 2 tablespoons garlic powder
- ¼ teaspoon cayenne pepper
- ½ teaspoon Stevia (liquid)

Directions:

1. Preheat your oven to 400 degrees Fahrenheit.
2. As the oven preheats, dry your wings using a paper towel then place them on a wire rack. Sprinkle them with sea salt and place them in the oven for 45 minutes.
3. After 45 minutes, turn your oven to broil and keep the wings in your oven for an additional 5 minutes, so they become nice and crisp.
4. As your wings bake, prepare the sauce. Combine the avocado oil, hot sauce, garlic powder, cayenne pepper, and liquid stevia in a blender. Blend until you have a smooth mixture then transfer to a large mixing bowl (the bowl needs to be large enough to hold all the wings as well).
5. Once the wings have come out of the oven, transfer them into the bowl with your sauce. Toss the wings so that they all get generously coated.

Nutrition:
Calories: 498| Carbs: 4g | Fat: 39g | Protein:30g

CHICK-FIL-A'S CHICKEN NUGGETS

Preparation Time: 10 minutes plus 2 hours for chilling
Cooking Time: 20 minutes
Servings: 1/5 recipe
Ingredients:

- 2 eggs
- 2 tablespoons heavy cream
- 1-pound chicken breast (cut into 1-inch pieces)
- 1 ½ cups panko breadcrumbs
- ½ cup pickle juice
- ½ teaspoon garlic powder
- ¼ teaspoon paprika
- ½ teaspoon Himalayan sea salt
- ¼ teaspoon black pepper

Directions:

1. Place your 1-inch cut chicken pieces into a sealable plastic bag. Pour in the pickle juice, seal the bag, and shake to ensure the chicken is well coated with the juice. Place the bag into the refrigerator for 2 hours.
2. When ready, preheat your oven to 425 degrees Fahrenheit. Then, line a baking sheet with parchment paper. Set the baking sheet to the side.
3. Take a medium-sized mixing bowl and combine the panko breadcrumbs, garlic powder, paprika, sea salt, and black pepper. Use a fork to mix everything together, then transfer to a sealable plastic bag and set to the side.
4. Take another medium-sized bowl and crack your eggs into it. Add in the heavy cream and beat together with a fork. Take your chicken pieces out of the refrigerator and transfer into the egg mixture. Make sure each piece gets well coated with the egg mixture.
5. Next, use tongs to transfer the chicken from the egg mixture to the plastic bag with the breadcrumbs. Give the bag a few shakes and gently press the breadcrumbs into the chicken pieces. When the chicken looks evenly coated, remove them from the bag and place them on a roasting rack set on top of your lined baking sheet. Place the chicken into the oven and bake for 20 minutes.
6. Once the chicken is a crispy golden color remove from the oven and serve.

Nutrition:
Calories: 261 | Carbs: 1g | Fat: 9.5g | Protein: 44.5g

MELLOW MUSHROOM'S PIZZA HOLY SHIITAKE

Preparation Time: 10 minutes
Cooking Time: 25 minutes
Servings: 1 square
Ingredients:

- 3 tablespoons truffle oil
- 1 tablespoon butter (melted)
- 3 cups mozzarella cheese
- 4 tablespoons cream cheese
- 1 ½ cups almond flour (alternative: coconut flour flaxseed)
- 2 tablespoons baking powder
- 2 tablespoons Swerve sweetener
- 2 egg
- Toppings:
- 1 cup mozzarella cheese (shredded)
- 2 cups baby bella mushrooms (sliced thin)
- ¼ cup oyster mushrooms (chopped)
- ¼ cup shiitake mushrooms (sliced)
- 1 sweet onion (diced)
- Aioli Sauce:
- ¾ cup mayo
- 3 garlic cloves (minced)
- 3 tablespoons lemon juice
- ½ teaspoon Himalayan sea salt
- ½ teaspoon black pepper

Directions:

1. Begin by preheating your oven to 425 degrees Fahrenheit, then line a baking sheet with parchment paper and set to the side.
2. As the oven preheats, prepare your dough. Take a large, microwave-safe bowl and add in your 3 cups of mozzarella and cream cheese. Place the bowl in the microwave and heat for 1 minute. Stir and heat again for 30 seconds. Keep an eye on the mixture; you just want the cheese to melt and become properly incorporated, not burn.
3. Once the cheese is melted, add in the eggs, almond flour, baking powder, and sweetener. Begin to mix everything together using a fork; it may become easier to use your hands once a dough begins to form.
4. Transfer the dough to your prepared baking sheet. Flatten the dough so that it stretches across the sheet or makes a rectangular shape. If the dough is too sticky, run your hands under cool water to help keep the dough from sticking to your fingers.

5. Once the dough is flattened out, use a fork to poke a few holes into the dough. Place the baking sheet into your oven and bake for 8 minutes. After 8 minutes remove your crust from the oven. If there are any bubbles in the crust, use a fork to pop them.
6. Take a small bowl and whisk together your truffle oil and melted butter. Then brush the mixture over the baked crust. Return the crust to the oven and bake for an additional 10 minutes.
7. As the crust continues to bake, prepare your toppings. Place a saucepan on your stove and turn the heat to medium. Add in your onions and sauté them until they turn a golden-brown color. Add your baby bella, shiitake, and oyster mushrooms to the pot. Allow the mushrooms to cook for 3 minutes, then turn off the heat.
8. Once your crust has turned a nice golden-brown color, remove it from the oven. Sprinkle your mozzarella cheese over the top then pour the mushroom mixture over the cheese. Return the pizza to the oven and bake for 3 more minutes or until the cheese has melted. Remove the pizza from the oven and allow it to cool slightly.
9. As the pizza cools, prepare your aioli sauce. Take a small mixing bowl and stir together the mayonnaise, minced garlic cloves, lemon juice, sea salt, and black pepper. Drizzle your sauce over the pizza then cut into 16 equal squares and serve.

Nutrition:
Calories: 219 | Carbs: 3.5g | Fat: 21g | Protein: 6g

WENDY'S CHILI

Preparation Time: 10 minutes
Cooking Time: 1 hour 45 minutes
Servings: 1/8 recipe
Ingredients:

- 3 pounds ground beef
- 2 teaspoons erythritol (granulated)
- 2/3 cups celery (diced)
- ½ cup red bell pepper (diced fine)
- ½ cup green bell pepper (diced fine)
- 1 ½ cups yellow bell pepper (diced fine)
- 1 cup tomatoes (diced)
- 1 ½ cups tomato juice
- 1 15-ounce can crushed tomatoes in purée
- 3 tablespoons Worcestershire sauce
- 3 tablespoons chili powder
- 1 teaspoon garlic powder
- 1 teaspoon cumin
- ½ teaspoon oregano (dried)
- 1 teaspoon Himalayan sea salt
- ½ teaspoon black pepper

Directions:

1. Take a large stockpot and place it on your stove; turn the heat to medium high to warm. Add your ground beef into the pot and allow it to cook for about 10 minutes or until it has all properly cooked and is a deep brownish color. Stir the meat regularly to avoid any large clumps of meat from forming. Once the ground beef has cooked, drain the excess oil, leaving about 2 tablespoons in the pot.
2. Add the onions, celery, red, green, and yellow bell pepper, and diced tomatoes. Stir and let the peppers cook for 5 minutes.
3. Next, pour in the tomato juice, crushed tomatoes, and Worcestershire sauce. Stir and allow the liquid to simmer for 3 minutes.
4. Add in the chili powder, garlic powder, cumin, oregano, sea salt, and black pepper to the pot. Stir, reduce the heat to medium, cover, and allow everything to cook for 1 hour.
5. After an hour stir, uncover, and cook for another 30 minutes over medium-low heat.
6. Turn off the heat and allow the chili to sit for about 10 minutes then ladle into bowls, top with your favorite toppings, and enjoy!

Nutrition:
Calories: 362 | Carbs: 3g | Fat: 11g | Protein: 53g

TRADITIONAL WINGS AND CELERY STICKS- BUFFALO WILD WINGS

Preparation Time: 25 minutes **Cooking Time:** 10-12 minutes **Servings:** 24 wings

Ingredients:

- Buffalo Wing sauce (Frank's Red Hot): 1 cup
- Cooking oil neutral (similar to avocado oil): 1/3 cup
- Granulated sugar: 1 tsp
- Garlic powder: 1 tsp
- Ground black pepper: 1/2 tsp
- Ground cayenne pepper: 1/2 tsp
- Worcestershire sauce: 1/2 tsp
- Water: 2 tsp
- Cornstarch: 2 tsp
- Egg yolk: 1
- To taste Kosher salt
- Chicken wings: 2 dozen
- For frying Neutral oil, like canola oil or avocado oil

Directions:

1. Red Hot Frank's sauce, granulated sugar, cooking oil, black pepper, garlic powder, Worcestershire sauce, and cayenne pepper into a medium saucepan. Bring the saucepan to medium heat to a boil until it bubbles, around 5 minutes. Adjust heat to a cooler.
2. In a small tub, whisk together water and the corn starch. The saucepan is attached to contents and cook the mixture until it is thick for 5 minutes.
3. The pan is removed from heat and set aside for about 10 min to cool.
4. When cooled, the sauce. Add a medium-size bowl with the yolk of the egg. In a steady stream to the yolk cooled sauce is added slowly, whisking continuously as you add, an emulsion is created so the oil is prevented from separating. The bowl contains when all of the sauce, cover the pot.
5. When the wings are immediately fried, the sauce is stored around room temperature till it's ready for usage. Hold the sauce in the fridge to keep it more than an hour. Taking it off towards counter just before wings frying.
6. Using a kitchen shear package or to cut the wing end a sharp knife, to clean the wings. To build two bits, discard the wingtip and now slice between the drumette and flat.
7. The wings are spiced with a sprinkling of salt.
8. In a big Dutch oven, heat around oil three inches in the meantime. Fill the machine to its MAX line if tabletop fryer (electric) is used.
9. The oil is preheated over medium-high to 350 degrees F, the deep-frying meter is used for temperature tests. Once at 350 degrees oil is reached, the heat is reduced to med-low.
10. The wings are dropped in the oil and now fry till they are golden brown, for around 10 to 12 min, and cook through to 165o F indoor temperature.

11. You might not cook at once all of the wings, depending on the size of your fryer. When wings have finished frying, a towel-lined sheet of paper is removed so the extra grease is drained and at 350 degrees let recover the oil before the addition of more wings.
12. The wings are placed in a wide bowl when the wings are all cooked. 1/3 to 1/2 cup is added of sauce and with tongs pairs spray the wings till well coated they are. If some leftover sauce you have, store it for around a week in the refrigerator, sealed.
13. The wings are served straight away as sauce makes the soggy coating.

Nutrition:
Calories: 685 | Carbs: 4g | Fat: 52g | Protein: 47g

CHAPTER 9

KETO COMPATIBLE VEGETABLE SIDES

COLESLAW

Preparation time: 5 minutes;
Cooking time: 0 minutes;
Serving: 6
Ingredients

- 14 ounces coleslaw mix
- 3 tablespoons erythritol sweetener
- ½ teaspoon celery salt
- ½ teaspoon ground black pepper
- 1 tablespoon apple cider vinegar
- 1 ½ tablespoon lemon juice
- 1 teaspoon mustard paste
- ¾ cup mayonnaise

Directions

- Take a large bowl, add all the ingredients in it except for coleslaw mix and then whisk until smooth.
- Add coleslaw mix, stir until well combined, and then taste to adjust the seasoning.
- Serve straight away.

Nutrition: 205 Cal; 20 g Fats; 1 g Protein; 2 g Net Carb; 2 g Fiber;

ZESTY ZUCCHINI CHIPS

Preparation time: 10 minutes;
Cooking time: 1 hour and 5 minutes;
Serving: 4
Ingredients

- 2 medium zucchini, ends trimmed
- 1 teaspoon of sea salt
- 2 tablespoons avocado oil

Directions

- Switch on the oven, then set it to 250 degrees F and let it preheat.
- Meanwhile, prepare the chips, and for this, cut them into thin slices.
- Take a baking sheet, line it with paper towels, spread zucchini slices in a single layer, sprinkle with salt, and then let them sit for 10 minutes.
- After 10 minutes, remove excess liquid from zucchini and then spread zucchini slices to a baking sheet lined with parchment paper.
- Brush the zucchini slices with oil and then bake for 45 to 65 minutes until crisp and nicely golden, turning halfway.
- When done, let chips cool for 5 minutes and then serve with dip.

Nutrition: 62 Cal; 7 g Fats; 0.2 g Protein; 0.2 g Net Carb; 0 g Fiber;

FAUXTATO CHIPS

Preparation time: 10 minutes;
Cooking time: 1 hour and 15 minutes;
Serving: 4
Ingredients

- 7 medium radishes, peeled, thinly sliced
- ½ teaspoon garlic powder
- 1 ½ teaspoon salt
- ¾ teaspoon ground black pepper
- 1 tablespoon avocado oil

Directions

- Switch on the oven, then set it to 225 degrees F and let it preheat.
- Prepare the radish and for this, peel them, cut them into thin slices, and then place the slices in a large bowl.
- Add garlic powder, salt, black pepper, and oil, toss until coated and then spread the radish slices in a single layer on a large baking sheet.
- Bake the radish chips for 1 hour and 15 minutes until crisp and nicely golden, turning halfway.
- When done, let chips cool for 5 minutes and then serve with dip.

Nutrition: 32 Cal; 3.4 g Fats; 0.1 g Protein; 0.1 g Net Carb; 0.1 g Fiber;

VEGETARIAN PIZZA

Preparation time: 10 minutes;
Cooking time: 20 minutes;
Serving: 8
Ingredients

- ½ cup baby spinach
- 1 cauliflower crust
- 1 tablespoon avocado oil

Directions

- Switch on the oven, then set it to 425 degrees F and let it preheat.
- Meanwhile, prepare the crust as instructed on its packet and then place it over a baking sheet or pizza pan.
- Drizzle oil over the crust, spread the spinach on top and then bake for 20 minutes until the crust turns nicely brown.
- When done, let the pizza cool for 5 minutes, then cut it into eight wedges and serve.

Nutrition: 44 Cal; 4 g Fats; 1 g Protein; 1 g Net Carb; 0.2 g Fiber;

MAC AND CHEESE

Preparation time: 10 minutes; **Cooking time**: 35 minutes; Serving: 6

Ingredients

- 1 large head of cauliflower
- 1/8 teaspoon garlic powder
- ½ teaspoon salt
- ¼ teaspoon ground black pepper
- 1 ½ teaspoons mustard paste
- 2 ounces cream cheese, cut into small pieces
- 1 ½ cup shredded cheddar cheese, divided
- 1 cup heavy cream

Directions

- Cut the cauliflower head into small florets, place them in a large heatproof bowl, and then it with a plastic wrap. Place the bowl into the microwave oven and then heat to for 10 to 15 minutes until florets have turned tender-crisp.
- Meanwhile, take a medium baking dish and grease it with oil.
- Drain the cauliflower florets, pat dry with paper towels and then transfer them into the prepared baking dish.
- Prepare the sauce and for this, take a small saucepan, place it over medium heat, add cream and then bring it to a simmer.
- Whisk in mustard and cream cheese until smooth, stir in garlic powder, salt, black pepper, and 1 cup of cheddar cheese and whisk well until the cheese has melted.
- Pour the sauce over cauliflower florets, spread remaining cheese on top and then bake for 15 minutes until the mixture bubbles and the top turns golden brown.
- When done, let mac and cheese cool for 5 minutes and then serve.

Nutrition: 316.8 Cal; 26.8 g Fats; 10.3 g Protein; 6 g Net Carb; 2.8 g Fiber;

CHAPTER 10

KETO COMPATIBLE SALADS

BRUSSELS SPROUT N' KALE SALAD

Preparation Time: 10 minutes
Cooking time: 1 minutes
Servings: 3
Ingredients:

- 1 bunch kale
- 1 pound Brussels sprouts
- 1/4cup craisins (or dry cranberries)
- 1/2cup pecans, chopped
- Maple vinaigrette
- 1/2cup olive oil
- 1/4cup apple cider vinegar
- 1/4cup maple syrup
- 1 teaspoon dry mustard

Directions

1. Slice the kale and Brussels sprouts with a cheese grater or mandolin slicer. Transfer to a salad bowl.
2. Add the pecans to a skillet on high heat. Toast for 60 seconds, then transfer to the salad bowl.
3. Add the craisins.
4. Mix all of the ingredients for the vinaigrette and whisk to combine.
5. Pour the vinaigrette over the salad and toss. Refrigerate for a few hours or preferably overnight before serving.

Nutrition:

Calories 135

Protein 35

Carbs 6

Fat 5

OLIVE GARDEN TOMATO, CUCUMBER AND ONION SALAD
Preparation Time: 10 minutes
Cooking time: 0 minutes
Servings: 3
Ingredients:
- 1 pound grape tomatoes
- 3 cucumbers, sliced
- 1/2cup white onion, sliced thinly
- 1 cup white vinegar
- 2 tablespoons Italian dressing
- 1/2cup sugar

Directions:
1. Whisk together the vinegar, sugar, and Italian dressing in a small bowl.
2. Add the cucumbers, tomatoes, and onions. Toss to coat. Cover with plastic wrap and refrigerate until ready to serve or for at least 1 hour before serving.

Nutrition:
Calories 218,
Total Fat 90 g,
Carbs 6 g,
Protein 39 g,
Sodium 2038 mg

CHAPTER 11

KETO COMPATIBLE DRESSINGS

CHICK-FIL-A SAUCE

Preparation time: 5 minutes; **Cooking time**: 0 minutes; Serving: 4
Ingredients

- ¼ teaspoon onion powder
- ¼ teaspoon garlic salt
- ½ tablespoon yellow mustard
- ¼ teaspoon smoked paprika
- ½ tablespoon stevia extract, powdered
- 1 teaspoon liquid smoke
- ½ cup mayonnaise

Directions

- Plug in a food processor, add all the ingredients in it, cover with the lid and then pulse for 30 seconds until smooth.
- Tip the sauce into a bowl and then serve.
  Nutrition: 183 Cal; 20 g Fats; 0 g Protein; 0 g Net Carb; 0 g Fiber;

118

BURGER SAUCE

Preparation time: 5 minutes;
Cooking time: 0 minutes;
Serving: 12
Ingredients

- 1 tablespoon chopped gherkin
- ½ teaspoon chopped dill
- ¾ teaspoon onion powder
- ¾ teaspoon garlic powder
- 1/8 teaspoon ground white pepper
- 1 teaspoon mustard powder
- ½ teaspoon erythritol sweetener
- ¼ teaspoon sweet paprika
- 1 teaspoon white vinegar
- ½ cup mayonnaise

Directions

- Take a medium bowl, place all the ingredients for the sauce in it and then stir until well mixed.
- Place the sauce for a minimum of overnight in the refrigerator to develop flavors and then serve with burgers.

Nutrition: 15 Cal; 7 g Fats; 0 g Protein; 0 g Net Carb; 0 g Fiber;

POLLO TROPICAL'S CURRY MUSTARD SAUCE

Preparation time: 5 minutes;
Cooking time: 0 minutes;
Serving: 12
Ingredients

- 2 teaspoon curry powder
- 4 teaspoons mustard paste
- 8 tablespoons mayonnaise

Directions

- Plug in a food processor, add all the ingredients in it, cover with the lid and then pulse for 30 seconds until smooth.
- Tip the sauce into a bowl and then serve.

Nutrition: 66 Cal; 7 g Fats; 1 g Protein; 0 g Net Carb; 1 g Fiber;

EL FENIX CHILI GRAVY

Preparation time: 5 minutes;
Cooking time: 40 minutes;
Serving: 28
Ingredients

- 2 tablespoons coconut flour
- ½ teaspoon salt
- ½ teaspoon ground black pepper
- 1/2 teaspoon dried Mexican oregano leaves
- 1 ½ teaspoon garlic powder
- 2 teaspoons ground cumin
- ½ teaspoon ground coriander
- 2 tablespoons oat fiber
- 2 tablespoons red chili powder
- 1/8 teaspoon dried thyme leaves
- ¼ cup lard
- 2 cups beef broth

Directions

- Take a medium skillet pan, place it over medium heat, add lard and when it melts, stir in flour, and then cook for 3 to 5 minutes until nicely browned, frequently lifting the pan from heat to cool slightly and then bring it back onto the fire.
- Stir in oat fiber, garlic, thyme, oregano, cumin, and coriander until mixed and cook for 2 minutes until it gets thick, stirring constantly.
- Then whisk in the broth until smooth, switch heat to the low level, and simmer the gravy fo3 30 minutes until sauce thickens.
- Remove pan from heat and serve.

Nutrition: 22 Cal; 2 g Fats; 0 g Protein; 0 g Net Carb; 0 g Fiber;

SWEET AND SMOKY CHIPOTLE VINAIGRETTE

Preparation time: 5 minutes;
Cooking time: 0 minutes;
Serving: 32
Ingredients

- 1 teaspoon garlic powder
- 1 teaspoon cumin
- 1 tablespoon salt
- 1 ½ tablespoon ground black pepper
- 1 teaspoon oregano leaves
- 1/3 cup liquid stevia
- ½ cup red wine vinegar
- 1 ½ cups avocado oil
- 1 tablespoon adobo sauce
- 1 tablespoon water

Directions

- Plug in a food processor, add all the ingredients in it except for oil, cover with the lid and then pulse for 30 seconds until smooth.
- Blend in oil in a steady stream until emulsified and then pour the salad dressing into a medium bowl.
- Serve straight away.
-
- Nutrition: 103 Cal; 11.5 g Fats; 0.05 g Protein; 3.05 g Net Carb; 0.05 g Fiber;

BANG BANG SAUCE

Preparation time: 5 minutes;
Cooking time: 0 minutes;
Serving: 6
Ingredients

- ¼ cup mayonnaise
- 1 ½ tablespoon garlic chili sauce
- 1 tablespoon rice vinegar
- 2 tablespoons monk fruit Sweetener
- 1/8 teaspoon salt

Directions

- Plug in a food processor, add all the ingredients in it, cover with the lid and then pulse for 30 seconds until smooth.
- Tip the sauce into a bowl and then serve.
  Nutrition: 90 Cal; 10 g Fats; 0 g Protein; 1 g Net Carb; 0 g Fiber;

SWEET CHILI SAUCE

Preparation time: 5 minutes;
Cooking time: 15 minutes;
Serving: 6

Ingredients

- 1 tablespoon garlic chili sauce
- ½ cup of water
- 2 scoops of beef bone broth collagen
- ¼ cup unseasoned rice vinegar
- 1 ½ teaspoon minced garlic
- ¼ teaspoon ground ginger
- ¼ cup erythritol sweetener
- 1 tablespoon avocado oil

Directions

- Take a large bowl, place all the ingredients in it except for oil and then whisk well until well combined.
- Take a medium saucepan, place it over medium heat, add sauce mixture and then simmer it for 15 minutes until the sauce has thickened.
- When done, remove the pan from heat, stir in oil, let the sauce cool completely and then serve.
  Nutrition: 25 Cal; 2.2 g Fats; 0 g Protein; 1.2 g Net Carb; 0 g Fiber;

BIG MAC SAUCE

Preparation time: 5 minutes;
Cooking time: minutes;
Serving: 6
Ingredients

- 1 tablespoon diced white onion
- 2 tablespoons diced pickles
- 1 teaspoon erythritol sweetener
- 1 tablespoon ketchup, low-carb
- 1 teaspoon dill pickle juice
- ½ cup mayonnaise

Directions

- Take a small bowl, place all of its ingredients in it and then stir well until incorporated.
- Serve straight away or store the sauce in an air-tight container.
  Nutrition: 138 Cal; 16 g Fats; 0 g Protein; 1 g Net Carb; 0.1 g Fiber;

CHAPTER 12

KETO COMPATIBLE SOUPS

MINESTRONE SOUP LIKE OLIVE GARDEN'S
Preparation Time: 15 minutes **Cooking Time:** 45 minutes **Servings:** 8
Ingredients:
- 3 tablespoons olive oil
- 1 cup minced white onion
- 1/2 cup chopped zucchini
- 1/2 cup frozen cut Italian cut green beans
- 1/4 cup minced celery
- 4 teaspoons minced garlic
- 4 cups vegetable broth (no substitutions)
- 2 (15 ounce) cans red kidney beans, drained
- 2 (15 ounce) cans small white beans, drained
- 1 (14 ounce) can diced tomatoes
- 1/2 cup carrot (julienned or shredded)
- 2 tablespoons minced fresh parsley
- 1 1/2 teaspoons dried oregano
- 1 1/2 teaspoons salt
- 1/2 teaspoon ground black pepper
- 1/2 teaspoon dried basil - 1/4 teaspoon dried thyme
- 3 cups hot water
- 4 cups fresh baby spinach
- 1/2 cup small shell pasta

Directions:
1. Heat three tablespoons of olive oil over medium heat in a large soup pot.
2. Sauté onion, celery, garlic, green beans, and zucchini in the oil for 5 minutes or until onions begin to turn translucent.
3. Add vegetable broth to pot, plus drained tomatoes, beans, carrot, hot water, and spices.
4. Bring soup to a boil, then reduce heat and allow to simmer for 20 minutes.
5. Add spinach leaves and pasta and cook for an additional 20 minutes or until desired consistency.

Nutrition: Calories: 1114 | Carbs: 19.45g | Fat: 118.47g | Protein: 5.13g

BROCCOLI CHEESE SOUP
Preparation Time: 10 minutes
Cooking Time: 30 minutes
Servings: 4
Ingredients:
- 1/6 cup butter
- ½ yellow onion, chopped
- 2 cloves garlic, finely chopped
- 1/6 cup almond flour
- 1 cup chicken stock
- 1 ½ cups half-and-half cream
- ¼ teaspoon salt
- ¼ teaspoon cracked black pepper
- ½ teaspoon vegetable stock powder
- ½ teaspoon mustard powder
- ½ teaspoon garlic powder
- ½ lb. broccoli florets, cut into small pieces
- 1 large carrot, peeled and grated
- 1 cup low-fat sharp cheddar cheese

Directions:
1. Use a suitable Dutch oven or a large pot and place it over medium heat.
2. Add butter to the Dutch oven and melt it on this heat.
3. Stir onion and sauté for 2 minutes until soft.
4. Add garlic and sauté for 1 minute.
5. Slowly add almond flour to the garlic and stir-fry until it turns golden brown.
6. Reduce the stove's heat to medium-low then pour in the chicken stock.
7. Slowly add the half and half cream to the soup and mix until it forms a lump-free mixture.
8. Add salt, black pepper, garlic powder, stock powder, and mustard powder.
9. Cook this mixture and adjust seasoning with salt and black pepper if needed.
10. Cook the soup for 5 minutes with occasional stirring.
11. Now add carrots and broccoli to the soup and cook the soup on a simmer for 20 minutes.
12. Once the broccoli is tender, add cheese to the soup.
13. Mix until the cheese is melted.
14. Garnish as desired. Serve warm.

Nutrition:
Calories: 369 | Carbs: 10.3g | Fat: 30.2g | Protein: 13.2g

FRENCH ONION SOUP

Preparation Time: 10 minutes
Cooking Time: 30 minutes
Servings: 2
Ingredients:

- 1medium onion, sliced
- 1 tablespoon butter
- 2 Teaspoons of swerve
- 1 Teaspoon Worcestershire sauce
- 1 1/3 cup broth
- 1 tablespoon of white wine
- Black pepper, ground, to taste
- 1/3 cup Swiss cheese, grated
- 3 tablespoons parmesan, grated

Directions:

1. Sauté onion with butter in a saucepan until brown.
2. Stir in Worcestershire sauce and swerve then cook for 13 minutes until the onions are completely caramelized.
3. Add black pepper, wine, and stock then boil the mixture.
4. Cook the onion soup for 15 minutes.
5. Divide the soup in the serving bowls and top them with cheese.
6. Broil the soup to melt the cheese on top.
7. Serve warm.

Nutrition: Calories: : 311 Carbs: 9g Fats: 20.7g Protein: : 22.3g

CONCLUSION

The most important advantage of using copycat restaurant recipes is that you can save money, but you can customize recipes if necessary. For example, if you want to reduce the salt or butter in one of the dishes, you can do it. Now you save money and at the same time provide a nutritious meal for your family.

You have little control over food ingredients when you eat out. You cannot personalize the dish you order because the sauces, etc. prepared in advance.

We all know that it is expensive to take your family out to dinner and can undoubtedly quickly throw a hundred bucks on the table. With copycat restaurant recipes, the same $ 100 can immediately produce four or more meals.

Now, imagine having all the necessary ingredients at home for a second to cook the same dish as a restaurant. So, when you create a restaurant recipe, you can "impress" your family and guests.

It will ask them to think they dined at a favorite restaurant using these recipes and saving money compared to food.

Trying to guess what the ingredients are in your favorite restaurant's food is eliminated when you use copycat recipes. Follow the recipes and slowly recreate your favorite food.

By having regular meals inspired by your favorite restaurants as a family, you can create a healthier and closer family. Research has shown that at school, families who dine together at home are closer, happier, and children perform better.

In short, the huge savings you get from cooking at home could be used for more productive things like family vacations or tuition for your children.

Going out to your favorite restaurant is always fun for most people. But what if you had access to the secret restaurant recipes that protect these restaurants so intensely? Will you go home cooking when you want?

It is not so difficult to learn to cook secret restaurant recipes. Some people think you need a degree in culinary arts or cooking to cook these secret recipes. I hate to tell you this, but anyone can collect the ingredients and cook a fancy meal that tastes like real. But do top-secret restaurant recipes prove the way the chef is served? Perhaps. You can quickly cook your favorite recipes with a little practice and patience.

The advantage of creating your own secret is that you can add its flavors and spices to your recipes. You would like to cook the basic formula and start adding what you think will improve the taste of the recipe after a while.

Cooking secret restaurant recipes will make your friends and family wonder where you learned how to cook so well. Imagine cooking a complete meal that looks like restaurant food. Certainly, some of your friends won't even believe you cooked it!

All of these dishes are custom-tested and customer-approved restaurants. Do you have an enjoyable meal at a restaurant and would like to replicate it at home? There are a few cloned restaurant recipes now because some of you have been asking for them. Almost every one of us went to a restaurant and had a meal that was so delicious that we wanted to know how to make that meal at home. There is a staggering increase in interest in discovering online restaurants.

Cooking also shows that there is no shortcut to performance. Now, I will create my meals and present them whenever I cook. Getting into the habit of eating at home is hard, but learning how to prepare your beloved restaurant meals in the luxury of your kitchen can make it a little easier. It's not that hard to learn how to cook secret restaurant meals. People think you need a background in cooking or a degree in culinary arts to be able to cook those secret dishes. What better way to control the consistency of what you and your family shove into your mouth than by preparing your meals? Today, this remains the best reason to learn to cook: because you can.

Made in the USA
Monee, IL
30 October 2021